ENGLAND'S MARVELOUS
GOTHIC CATHEDRALS
AND
CHURCHES

Copyright © 2019 by Richard Moore and Sawon Hong.
All rights reserved.

No part of this book may be reproduced, stored in a retrieval system,
or transmitted by any means, without the written permission of the author.

ISBN: 978-0-578-43004-1 (print)
ISBN: 978-0-578-42006-5 (e-book)

Cover photo: Scissor arches, Wells Cathedral

ENGLAND'S MARVELOUS GOTHIC CATHEDRALS AND CHURCHES

Richard Moore and Sawon Hong

Timeline of Key Events Related to English Gothic Churches

HISTORICAL EVENTS	DATE/PERIOD	ARCHITECTURAL DEVELOPMENTS
Anglo-Saxon period	5th century to 1066	
Augustine papal mission spreads Christianity	597 CE	Saxon church building
Norman conquest	1066	Period of Norman church construction
Thomas Becket's murder	1170	
	1175	Introduction of Gothic design in Canterbury Cathedral
	1190–1530	**English Gothic design periods**
	1190–1250	Early Gothic period
	1250–1340	Decorated period
	1340–1530	Perpendicular period
Reformation and dissolution of monasteries	1536–1541	
Oliver Cromwell's Civil War	1642–1651	
	18th to 21st centuries	Period of restoration, renovation, and repair

Table of Contents

Preface 7

PART ONE: Backdrop of Gothic Cathedrals and Churches in England

Historical Background 11
Pre-Gothic Church Architecture 14
From Norman to Gothic Architecture 15
Arrival of English Gothic 22
England's Three Gothic Periods 23
Building a Gothic Church 25

PART TWO: Profiles of Selected Gothic Cathedrals and Churches

Selection Criteria 29
Church Orientation 29

LONDON AND SOUTHEAST
Westminster Abbey 31
Canterbury Cathedral 44
Winchester Cathedral 58

EAST
King's College Chapel, Cambridge 71
Ely Cathedral 80
Peterborough Cathedral 92

NORTHEAST
Lincoln Cathedral 105
York Minster 118
Durham Cathedral 130

SOUTHWEST
Gloucester Cathedral 143
Wells Cathedral 154
Exeter Cathedral 166
Salisbury Cathedral 178

Annexes
Practical Information for Visitors 189
Glossary of Terms 190
References 194
Image Sources and Attribution 196
Acknowledgements 197

Peterborough Cathedral and gate

PREFACE

England's Marvelous Gothic Cathedrals and Churches

Given our passion for history, architecture, and art, we always visit old religious buildings wherever we travel. Over the years, our particular interest became more focused on Gothic cathedrals.

What is it about these church buildings from medieval times that makes them so addictive? Medieval churches are by their nature spiritual places, steeped in history, and hotbeds of religious passion. They all record the stories of people and events that began many hundreds of years ago. While that is true, only Gothic churches are complex, are full of light, have beautiful windows and decorative features, and have unique architecture. Visiting them stimulates our sense of the past and our imagination. We feel so fortunate to have "discovered" these special buildings and want to share our experiences with others.

Since we were more familiar with France, we started with our guide to selected French Gothic Cathedrals. While researching the French guidebook we continually ran across references to what was going on across the Channel in England during the Gothic period. We ended up with a good deal of fragmentary knowledge about English Gothic churches, together with a growing interest. These influences evolved into the writing this guidebook.

This book is addressed especially to those who are curious about the story behind English Gothic churches, and who would like information ranging from some history of each to their architectural and other highlights. That is, visitors who would like to have some understanding of what they are seeing during their visits without getting bogged down with masses of personages, technical details, and tiresome lists of all the changes and renovations done in each church over the centuries.

What we found most distinctive and spectacular in the English Gothic churches are the ceilings: their intricate designs, subtle colors, scale, and diversity. There are two basic types of ceilings. The first is found throughout the main areas of the church, which has four main styles: basic ribbing, complex ribbing, fan vaulting, and rarer wooden ceilings. Four examples of the first type ceiling are:

Basic rib, Wells   Complex rib, York   Fan-vault, Peterborough   Wood, Ely

The second type is the ceiling found under the crossing tower in many cathedrals.

Canterbury   Lincoln   York

While these excursions into the past are thrilling on so many levels, we are also pleased with the effort being made by church authorities to connect modern people to these architectural wonders. Seeking to be relevant in their local community, they host musical events, lectures, and fairs, and provide programs for school children—and much more. In keeping up with modern times, they also commission excellent new work. Some examples are: stained-glass windows by a contemporary British painter and stained-glass artist Thomas Denny (at Durham, Gloucester, and Salisbury); sculptures by Antony Gormley (at Winchester and Canterbury); and the contemporary baptismal font by William Pye (at Salisbury).

In addition to our own visits to each church listed in this book, we have consulted many sources. While it is helpful to have so much information, the inconsistencies among them have required much in-depth research. An additional challenge was that, given their architectural complexity, Gothic churches consist of many parts, each with its own timing and terminology. We have tried to simplify as much as possible without sacrificing key information. We have made an effort to reduce or eliminate the use of the more arcane terms with which few visitors will be familiar. To simplify the text, we have in many cases opted to use the generic term "church" instead of constantly shifting between the terms "cathedral, abbey, and chapel." A cathedral is a church that is the seat of a bishop.

"Transfiguration," Durham

Font, Salisbury

This guidebook is organized basically into two parts. Part One begins with background information about Gothic churches, including history and the evolution of architectural design in Europe and England. This part ends with an overview of England's unique approach to Gothic design. Part Two provides concise, illustrated profiles of each of the 13 churches which are the focus of this guidebook. Annexes include practical information for visitors, a glossary, list of references, and image sources.

10

Frieze, Canterbury

PART ONE

Backdrop of Gothic Cathedrals and Churches in England

Historical Background

During medieval times, life was precarious, even terrifying. The backdrop was one of fear, violence, bloodshed, brutality, starvation, death, and anxiety about one's fate after death. The average life expectancy of ordinary people was no more than 30 years. Throughout, drought, plague, war, and civil unrest recurred. Despite all the discomforts of life in the Middle Ages, these centuries gave us, among other things, printed books, eyeglasses, anesthetics, pets, glazed windows, underwear, playing cards, the fireplace, gunpowder, forks, and universities.

Belief System

In the Middle Ages, Heaven and Hell were not abstractions: the saints were holy and the devil was evil incarnate. Death and the afterlife—Heaven and Hell—were omnipresent, due in part to the frequency of violence, epidemics and malnutrition, as well as illness and death from accidents or from mysterious causes. These were the fixtures of everyday life. The firm belief in miracles created a demand for religious relics of all kinds. And this helps explain the power of relics and the importance of pilgrimages conducted to seek the fulfillment of wishes or even miracles. Inner life was totally influenced by a belief in magic and witchcraft as well as the spirit world. People considered, for instance, cats as agents of witchcraft and incarnations of Satan. As the story goes, they slaughtered so many cats that the rodent population exploded, which is said to have facilitated the spread of the Black Plague.

While people were often critical of the Church and churchmen, they needed them to act as their intermediary with God—a belief that fit nicely with the raison d'être of the Church. The most revered Church figures were the saints, whose names and images are found everywhere, including in the names of churches.

A series of miracles and legends were attributed to these saints, and the pilgrims responded. The fame of their miracles—and relics—drew such large crowds of pilgrims that churches had to be expanded. The contributions of the multitudes helped pay for this.

How and Why Things Changed

Europe was overwhelmingly rural during the Middle Ages, and wealth was based upon land, not money. There was little commerce and few towns. Then, due to a number of developments around the year 1000, things started to change for the better, creating the basis for large undertakings, like building major churches.

TRADE AND WEALTH

Following the end of the Viking raids, the Anglo-Saxon incursions, and the Norman invasion in 1066, the establishment of order in Europe led to a growth of trade and wealth, and an associated growth in towns, which expanded dramatically in the 11th and 12th centuries. Despite these advances, subsistence agriculture continued to occupy 90 percent of the population.

FOOD AND POPULATION

It's important to realize how small the population of Western Europe was. In the year 1086, for instance, the total population of England was only about two million. The largest city, London, had only 18,000 people, while the average size of the towns was about 2,500. A period of warm weather increased food production and population growth. The prolonged warm spell was so supportive of agriculture that there were vineyards in southern and eastern England.

Setting for English Gothic Cathedrals and Churches

The English area of today's UK is where Gothic church architecture took hold. Geographically, England is small, covering only 50,000 square miles. It is, however, blessed with a relatively non-mountainous terrain, many rivers, an enormous shoreline, fertile soil, and a mild climate. All combined to assure an unusual potential for producing wealth from agriculture and trade, and to make it a magnet for ambitious outsiders. By the time of the Norman Conquest in 1066, the borders between England and the areas beyond—peopled by the Welsh (in the west) and Scots (in the north) and including, for a time, the Viking invaders who settled mainly in the Northeast and East—were reasonably defined, although often contested.

Christianity arrived in Britain via Roman traders and artisans around 43 CE, and was later endorsed by Emperor Constantine in about 313 CE. However, pagan beliefs were common and Christianity continued to be a minority faith. In 597 CE Pope Gregory in Rome sent the Benedictine Abbot Augustine as a missionary to Canterbury to establish a church and proselytize.

Until the reign of Henry VIII the Roman Catholic Church represented Christianity in England. Throughout the Middle Ages, there was little distinction between Church and State. While the pope looked after Church doctrine, bishops were responsible for their churches and abbots for their monasteries. These religious leaders also played an important governing role: overseeing towns and cities, and managing local taxation and administration. Under bishops and abbots, there were two distinct types of churchmen: secular clergy who worked with the laity; and monks or monastics who were secluded in monastic communities.

There were three models of churches: those run by secular clergy (non-monastic church), those run by monks (monastic church), and those run by a mix of secular clergy and monks. These three types of churches differed in other important ways as regards organization and finance, but not necessarily architecture.

Around 1300, catastrophe struck in the form of arctic-level climate change, closely followed by the Black Death, aka the Plague, in 1348–1349, which recurred several times. These double scourges resulted in a 50 percent loss of population, the collapse of the economy, and a major slowdown in church construction, which continued into the mid-16th century. During this time there were few major building projects, Salisbury and Wells Cathedrals being exceptions. As the population grew and the economy recovered, some parts of England, particularly the wool-growing and cloth-exporting areas, bounced back far more quickly than others.

In 1534, Parliament made Henry VIII the head of the Church in England, thus separating England from papal authority. Between 1536 and 1541, Henry VIII disbanded all monastic institutions and confiscated their income. As one source states: "The dissolution of the monasteries in the late 1530s was one of the most revolutionary events in English history. At the time there were roughly 900 religious houses in England: 260 for monks, 300 for regular canons, 142 nunneries, and 183 friaries. This act affected approximately 12,000 people: 4,000 monks, 3,000 canons, 3,000 friars and 2,000 nuns" (Bernard, 390). Reformation zealots also caused considerable damage to most churches, as did the later Civil War (1642–1651).

Today, there are 26 cathedrals in England that date between 1040 and 1540. They are highly diversified in style: with a few exceptions, a mix of Norman and Gothic. Only 16 of these had been cathedrals at the time of the Reformation, the rest were so designated later.

Pre-Gothic Church Architecture

After the Romans left England in about 410 CE the fundamentals of Roman basilica design would emerge as the dominant style of architecture. The Romans themselves left behind few stone buildings of interest, and none had immediate relevance to the design or construction of English Gothic churches. The most well-known of these constructions are the Roman bath complex in the city of Bath and Hadrian's Wall in the north.

From the mid-5th to early-7th centuries, Anglo-Saxon invaders from the western coasts of Europe wiped out many of the local communities and replaced them with their own settlements, and their kingdoms spread across most of England and parts of lowland Scotland. This marked a complete break with the past.

Church Building

In about 597 CE Abbot Augustine built the first English cathedral in Canterbury. More cathedrals followed at Rochester, London, and York. Within a hundred years, England had several hundred churches. Given the wholesale destruction of these Anglo-Saxon churches by the Normans, their design is not well-documented.

Among these was Winchester Cathedral (648 CE), which was considered the finest building in England at the time. Another major Anglo-Saxon church, Westminster Abbey (c. 1040), was built by Edward the Confessor using masons from Normandy, where he was brought up. It was the largest building in Northern Europe at the time. By the turn of the 10th century, the Anglo-Saxons had built some of the largest and most lavish buildings in Europe.

In 1070, Abbot Lanfranc, who was appointed Archbishop of Canterbury by William the Conqueror, collaborated with William to put the Catholic Church under government control. The Church quickly amassed a great deal of land, and bishops became men of wealth and power, which helped finance the massive surge in church building. By the time of Henry I's death in 1135, 16 of the 17 English ecclesiastical districts had a cathedral. This was the largest and most ambitious building program in English architectural history.

Influences on Church Design

One of the major influences on church design was the Romanesque church at Caen in Normandy, where Archbishop Lanfranc had been abbot. He even emulated the dimensions of the Caen Abbey. Architecturally, however, this did not signal a new type of architecture. Each of the 16 cathedrals was a mix of styles influenced by bishops, resources, and local traditions. In Medieval England, what came to be called Norman was heavily derivative of the Romanesque style in Europe. It is commonly known as Norman because the major building scheme in the 11th and 12th centuries was initiated by William the Conqueror. Accordingly, and to simplify things, in this book, we refer to the Romanesque influence on English medieval architecture as Norman.

Relics, especially the bodies of saints, also influenced church design. Since they were believed to have supernatural power and to serve as intermediaries with divine powers, pilgrims came to venerate them. Facilities needed to be added that could display the saints and accommodate the flow of pilgrims. The result was that churches were now divided into three sections: one for the clergy (the screened-off choir and high altar area at the east end); one for lay people (for services in the nave at the west end); and one for pilgrims (in the crypt, and in shrines at the east end).

From Norman to Gothic Architecture

One way to trace the evolution of English churches from Norman to Gothic is to begin with the differing visions that informed these two architectural styles. Sponsors of churches must have had a vision which informed the implementation. More a spirit than a defined style, the sponsors and builders were trying to achieve what the church would communicate, how it would actually function, and what it would look like, that is, its spiritual message, its practical requirements, and its aesthetics.

Origin and Vision of the Romanesque–Norman Architectural Styles

Roman basilicas were entirely non-religious. They were used for administering justice and for a range of commercial purposes. Basilica floor plans were rectangular, with side aisles, a raised apse, and a rounded east end. Piers (the supports between arcade openings) separated the center aisle from the side aisles. These piers support the walls and ceilings. The churches were heavily built and not high: The ceiling was not heavy and the walls were pierced with only a few, comparatively small, windows high up. There was, thus, little need for buttresses to support the building. These buildings were poorly illuminated, but they had wall space for paintings or even murals, and had decorated piers and other ornamentation. Early Christians adopted this design when they created their places of worship. Indeed, they often simply took over Roman basilicas!

Although the basilica design did evolve into the style known as Romanesque—in size and with the addition of transepts to create the cruciform floor plan—it remained the basis of church design. After the Norman Conquest, the derivative of Romanesque was called the Norman style. Like its Romanesque cousin, Norman architecture had heavy walls, round-topped arches, small windows, and simple ornamentation. The design was all about dignity and gravitas, a serious building built for serious purposes.

Origin and Vision of the Gothic Architectural Style

In one of history's great ironies, the term Gothic first appeared during the latter part of the Renaissance when it was used pejoratively to describe an architectural style considered rustic, coarse, and uncivilized. The term implied that, compared to superior, classical buildings, the Gothic medieval churches were so crude that only the Goths could have produced them. The Goths were a warlike Germanic tribe who played an important role in the fall of the Roman Empire and the emergence of Medieval Europe.

Abbot Suger of St Denis outside Paris is credited with a vision of his abbey church that was different from the Romanesque style. His vision was a church which would represent Heaven as a signpost and gateway to Paradise; it would be a church full of light as a metaphor for God. Suger set to work in about 1135 to convert his abbey church into a structure that would embody as much of this vision as possible. To achieve these goals would result in a different looking church: much taller and with thinner window-filled walls.

CREATE A PHYSICAL METAPHOR FOR HEAVEN
In contrast to the visual concept behind earlier Romanesque design, the Gothic emphasis was to create massive, light-filled, vertical spaces for worship as metaphors for Heaven. Gothic churches were the first designed to flood the interior with light.

CREATE AN ORGANICALLY UNIFIED WHOLE
Gothic style was also different from early church design in that it integrated all the elements of the building to create an organically unified whole. The ceilings and masses of windows created an interior space that was often spacious, soaring, and bright. Their sheer size—their width and length—ensured that they would feel expansive.

EMPHASIZE VERTICALITY
The ceilings reached great heights and were tied to the floor by half-round shafts (small, often rounded, features attached to or clustered around a pier). These shafts created a vertical line leading the eye upward from floor to ceiling.

It is of course impossible to know so many centuries later which came first: the vision, or the three Gothic architectural solutions needed to make the vision a reality. More generally, this transformative Gothic vision consisted of creating a physical metaphor for Heaven, creating a unified whole, and emphasizing verticality and height. The Gothic vision for a cathedral was very different from what went before, even revolutionary.

Basic Functions of a Gothic Church

To achieve the sponsors' vision of how a church would actually function and what it would look like, they were built to perform a mix of several functions. The most important of these were to provide an emotional, spiritual experience; generate support for the Church; provide religious lessons; and provide a practical venue for church and community activities.

PROVIDE AN EMOTIONAL, SPIRITUAL EXPERIENCE

The goal was to inspire, teach, and dazzle, meanwhile actively involving the community in the power and importance of religion (and the Church) in their lives in a variety of ways. One was to engage people and to connect them personally with a vision of a "New Jerusalem"—an image of Heaven. These churches were physical metaphors of the Christian faith directing the eye upward toward God. Their sculptures reinforced the Church's messages about salvation and damnation.

In other words, Gothic churches were deliberately designed as shock-and-awe experiences: wowing, humbling, and inspiring. Recent restoration activities show that originally many churches were richly decorated with paint and gilt, both inside and out. Sculpture and architectural details were often brightly colored.

GENERATE SUPPORT FOR THE CHURCH

Although the major functions of a church were to honor God and reinforce religion, the church was eager to enhance its power, influence, income, and image.

PROVIDE RELIGIOUS LESSONS

This function was achieved via sermons, Bible study windows, as well as carvings and statuary. Bible study windows played an essential role at a time when few people were literate.

PROVIDE A VENUE FOR CHURCH AND COMMUNITY ACTIVITIES

In the Middle Ages a church was: a place which often housed sacred relics to attract pilgrims and their contributions; an inspiring setting for religious rituals, plus other key functions, e.g., marriage, baptism, death rites; and as a venue for religious celebrations and saints days. The churches allowed all manner of commercial activities to take place in its precincts and also sponsored trade fairs. Many of these functions would act—at least in part—as income-generating activities.

Essential Features of Gothic Architecture

Achieving the vision of a taller, light-filled church meant much greater pressure on the thinner, window-filled walls, pushing them outward, and thereby threatening collapse. The architectural solutions were brought together for the first time by Abbot Suger in expanding his abbey. His solutions included three features essential to Gothic architecture: the pointed arch, the ribbed vault, and the flying buttress.

POINTED ARCH
This architectural feature is thought to have been first used in the Middle East in the early days of Islam. The advantage of a pointed arch over a round-topped arch is that it can support far more weight, thus reducing the thrust the ceiling exerted on the walls. This arch provided greater support to thinner walls.

RIBBED VAULT
The ribbing superstructure divides the stone "filling" between the ribs into smaller sections, resulting in a major reduction on the weight of the ceiling. Ribbed vaulting also channels the weight of the vault onto piers at the corners of each vault, instead of onto side walls.

FLYING BUTTRESS
The thinner, taller and window-filled walls need support to keep them stable in the face of high winds, movements of the earth, and settlement of a building over time. Each flying buttress is attached to a vertical buttress, or pier. It "flies" upward from a pier to intersect the exterior wall in order to support it. The most famous component is the flying buttress, but other buttress forms are attached directly to the walls, or act as hidden interior engineering supports.

The combination of these three elements had the revolutionary effect of allowing much higher ceilings and thinner walls, as well as the far greater window openings needed to illuminate the interior. These advances also allowed for installing windows higher up in the building's walls, especially the clerestory and the triforium, the two usually window-filled levels above the ground-floor arcade level.

Basic Architectural Features of Gothic Design
Nearly all pure and partly Gothic churches share the basic architectural features, both interior and exterior. In English churches, however, the horizontal features are more prominent than the vertical ones. That is, they tend to be longer and lower, in contrast to the French Gothic emphasis on verticality.

EXTERIOR

West Front, Transept Façades, and Portals English Gothic churches have two major styles for their west front: one is highly decorated and the other much less so. The former is called the "screen design," whose focus is horizontal, using multiple layers of niches filled with stone sculptures of biblical, ecclesiastical, and noble figures. Good examples are at Lincoln and Exeter. The latter less-decorated style emphasizes the west window and verticality, such as at York and Canterbury.

While there are two or three doorways on English west front and transept façades, they are almost always small and relatively undecorated compared to those in France.

Towers and Spires English churches typically have two, usually square, towers on the west end, while some have an additional central tower at the crossing. A small number also have a spire. Many towers are topped with pinnacles.

Buttresses While buttressing of all kinds is commonly used on English Gothic churches, it is rarely prominent. In many cases, buttressing is present—inside as well as outside—to protect major church features from collapsing due to the poor foundations found in some of England's churches.

INTERIOR

Nave, Aisles, and Vaults The central nave aisle is flanked by side aisles, usually one on each side of the nave, but sometimes there are two aisles on each side. The vaulted nave ceiling is much taller than the vaulted aisle ceilings. Half-round shafts often sweep unbroken from floor to ceiling and meet the ribs of the vaulted ceilings, like tall trees spreading their branches.

Although, like their French counterparts, English cathedrals initially had four- or six-part ribbed vaults, English ceilings evolved into increasingly complex designs, culminating in the elaborate and beautiful fan-vaulting style.

Elevation Most Gothic churches have a three-level interior elevation: the arcade (a row of arches on the ground floor supported by piers); the triforium (an arcaded–wall passage at the level of the aisle roof); and the clerestory (the topmost level of the nave, which is mostly glass). Depending on the church, the three levels may be given equivalent treatment, or one may be stressed at the expense of the others.

Transepts, Chapels, and East End A transept is an arm that crosses between the nave and choir at a right—north–south—angle. A transept extends outward from the north and south sides of the nave. Some churches have two transepts, and one or both may project beyond the walls. Chapels may also project beyond the walls, and most churches have a flat, rather than rounded, east end.

Visual Depiction of Architectural Features

The two drawings below—a floor plan and a cross-sectional profile—identify these common architectural features. Becoming familiar with their locations will help visitors follow the explanations in this guidebook more easily. The floor plan is viewed from above. The cross-sectional profile drawing shows a cathedral from the west end.

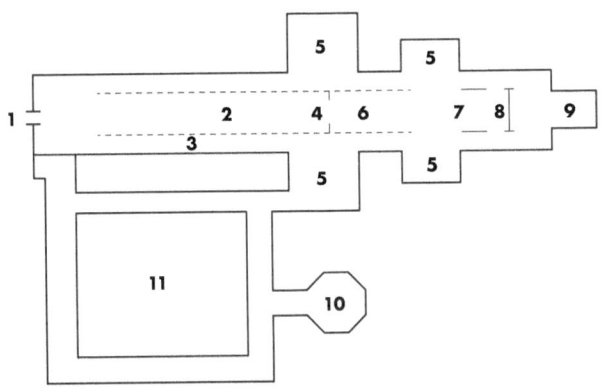

Architectural Features of Floor Plan

1. West front
2. Nave
3. Side aisle
4. Crossing
5. Transept
6. Choir
7. High altar
8. East end
9. Lady Chapel
10. Chapter house
11. Cloister

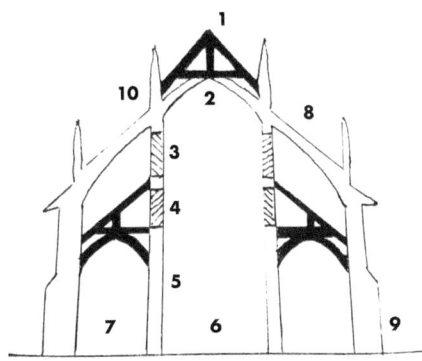

Architectural Features of Cross-section

1. Nave roof ceiling
2. Vault
3. Clerestory level
4. Triforium level
5. Arcade level
6. Nave
7. Side aisle
8. Flying buttress
9. Buttress pier
10. Pinnacle

Arrival of English Gothic

After the Norman invasion, Gothic architectural features arrived in England from Europe and superseded the Norman style. This new Gothic style was first known as "the French style." Elements of the new style were inserted into existing churches. Even before that, however, some features had been installed in Durham Cathedral by about 1104, with its combination of Norman and proto-Gothic styles. For example, masons at Durham experimented with ribbed vaulting before it was widely adopted elsewhere, even predating St Denis. By 1175, with the completion of the choir at Canterbury Cathedral by William of Sens, the Gothic style was firmly established in England.

England's Vision of Gothic Churches

While the Gothic vision was closely followed in Europe, especially in France, that was less the case in England. One reason is that the Normans quickly engaged in a massive building program of large and costly, essentially Norman-style, churches. Despite the French influence, English architects chose to freely interpret the application of these Gothic features and introduced innovations of their own. The English vision put far less emphasis on verticality, light, and a unified design than their European counterparts. The priority was instead heavily in favor of other characteristics, such as length, complex ceilings, elaborate chapels, and choir screens.

Are They Gothic?

Architecturally speaking, this differing focus in England meant a continued, but different, use of all three Gothic elements. For example, English architects placed great emphasis on pointed (i.e., lancet) windows as well as other openings, and on vaulting. For the reasons noted (e.g., lower wall height), they paid less attention to obvious buttressing. Much of the buttressing they did was to counteract subsidence of towers due to unstable foundations.

Given the resulting mix of Norman and Gothic in most English Gothic churches, one might ask whether English Gothic churches should instead be dubbed as "Norman-with-Gothic-features." However, rather than complicate things, we have chosen to refer to all the churches in this guidebook as "Gothic."

Special Attributes of English Gothic Churches

Despite the great variability in the features of English Gothic churches, there are a number of commonalities that distinguish them from their European counterparts. While not every church exhibits every characteristic, the following tend to be the most prevalent and significant.

EXTERIOR FEATURES
- Setting: It tends to be in a garden-like precinct which often includes other buildings related to the church.
- An emphasis on length rather than height: It affects the number of windows and diminishes the feeling of verticality.
- East end: It is often flat, rather than rounded.
- Large, central towers: They are set above the crossing.
- Chapter house and cloister: Elaborate versions are present (if not destroyed) even in some non-monastic churches.
- Transepts: The north and south extensions may project out from the side walls.
- Windows: West front, transept, and east end windows are generally pointed, as opposed to the round "rose" windows often seen in French cathedrals.

INTERIOR FEATURES
- Thick walls, smaller windows, and less-visible buttressing.
- Elaborate and complex rib-design ceilings, culminating in England's great contribution of fan vaulting.
- Often elaborate choirs with carved choir screens; decorated organs, sometimes set atop the choir screen; and a great deal of carving on the stalls and seats.

England's Three Gothic Periods

The English Gothic style can be divided into three periods: Early Gothic, Decorated, and Perpendicular. While these three periods are logical divisions, Gothic design is not easily broken into discrete time periods. Just as there was an overlap between the Norman and the Gothic styles, there were overlaps between the three Gothic periods. As fashions changed, new elements were often used alongside older ones, especially in large buildings such as churches, which were constructed (and added to) over long periods of time. Accordingly, one should treat most architectural dates offered herein as approximate.

Each period made full, although variable, use of all three essential features of Gothic architecture: pointed arches, various ceiling designs, and buttresses. Buttressing, not just the flying variety, but all forms, including internal "braces," were employed. They are in evidence, both outside and inside, where needed to support walls or to shore up unsteady towers. Examples of internal buttressing can be seen at Gloucester Cathedral, while well-known examples of bracing can be seen at Wells and Salisbury.

Early Gothic Period (c. 1190–1250)

The most characteristic feature of this period is the pointed arch. Such arch shapes were used throughout the early English churches, most noticeably in the pointed-arch windows. In addition, the walls were higher and the ceilings were constructed of vaulted stone. By contrast, Norman ceilings were often made of wood—perhaps architects were not sure how to span interior spaces using heavier stone. Fine examples of this wooden ceiling can be seen at Ely, Peterborough, and a few other English Gothic churches. The new style piers were clusters of slender shafts surrounding a central pier. Circles with trefoils and quatrefoils (ornamental designs of three, four, or five lobes or leaves, resembling a flower or four-leaf clover) were introduced into the window tracery. The carvings decorating the capitals are highly varied. With the completion of the choir at Canterbury Cathedral by William of Sens in 1175, the style was firmly established in England.

Decorated Period (c. 1250–1340)

The Decorated period mainly focused on elaborate stone window tracery. At first, this tracery was based on the trefoil and quatrefoil often combined to form netlike patterns. The Early Gothic lancet windows were replaced by windows of great width and height, divided by complex stone mullions (slender shaft or narrow column used to divide a window) and decorated with quatrefoils or other tracery decorations. The tracery evolved into the greater use of S-shaped curves, which creates flowing, flame-like forms. This period also emphasized elaborately carved capitals, often with floral patterns. The vaulting became increasingly elaborate where shorter ribs are connected to the main ribs to form a variety of patterns. In addition, in a few cases, decorative bosses (rounded caps often found at the intersection of ceiling ribs) were added.

The Decorated period produced experiments in tracery and vault design that anticipated by 50 years or more the similar emphases of the Flamboyant period in France.

Perpendicular Period (c. 1340–1530)

This period is called Perpendicular due to its emphasis on vertical lines. The elaborate tracery of the Decorated period was no longer emphasized, and the lines on both walls and windows have become sharper and less flamboyant. This perpendicular linearity is particularly obvious in the design of windows, which became very large, sometimes immense, with slimmer stone mullions, allowing greater scope for stained glass. Of special note is the artistic elaboration of the vaulting, which reached new highs of flamboyance with intricate multipartite vaults, and which culminated in fan vaulting. Piers continued to be surrounded by clusters of thin shafts, as was done during the Decorated period. The triforium disappeared, or was replaced with paneling, which emphasized the clerestory windows.

Building a Gothic Church

Once a decision was made to build a church in whichever design, more practical issues remained. How much would it cost? Who would pay? How long would it take?

Cost

It is difficult to gather information about what it cost to build a medieval church. There are many reasons for this: record-keeping in those days was poor; frequent fires destroyed records; most churches were built over a period of decades, or even centuries; funding usually came from more than one source; and at least part of the cost was met by in-kind donations of labor and material. Another problem is how to translate what something cost nearly a thousand years ago into today's money. Thus, cost estimates are highly approximate.

For example, Henry III's rebuilding of Westminster Abbey is considered "the most lavish act of religious architectural patronage by any one individual in the entire Middle Ages" (Scott, 36). By the time of his death in 1272, it had cost £45,000. To put this amount in perspective, the total income for Henry's entire realm during this period was only £35,000 per year. The abbey thus consumed five percent of the king's total wealth during the years of its construction. In today's money, £45,000 would be about £9 billion, not including the cost of the lavish Henry VII Lady Chapel added in the 16th century. Salisbury, without the spire, cost about £28,000 over 50 years. Calculations on the basis of wage rates suggest that the cost of each Gothic church would amount to "hundreds of millions of pounds in modern currency."

The major elements of the overall cost were for labor and materials. For example, at any given time the largest number of workers employed from May to end November in 1253 at Westminster Abbey was 435 (Scott, 32). The smallest number of seasonal workers was 119, with an average of 309. Recall that these labor costs would increase and continue for some part of 343 years in the case of Canterbury Cathedral. There were about two common laborers for every skilled person (Ibid, 30).

Sources of Funding

The main funding source was the Church, which was richly endowed, and occasionally kings (particularly in the cases of Westminster Abbey and King's College Chapel). As major centers of Norman power, they were able to acquire further lands formerly held by dispossessed landowners. Furthermore, the development of the tithe as a compulsory tax on agricultural production resulted in greatly increased incomes for incumbent clergy. The Church controlled one-third of the country's wealth before Henry VIII stripped it of much of its lands and privileges. By the end of the 13th century, 12 of Europe's 40 richest dioceses were in England. This wealth, carefully deployed by bishops and deans, paid for the lavishness of cathedrals like Salisbury and Lincoln.

Given the huge costs involved, Church sources alone weren't enough. So the churches engaged in a variety of fund-raising efforts, such as appeals for gifts, especially gifts of land. An effective strategy was to capitalize on a famous saint. To fill gaps in financing, even rich churches relied on money lenders. Despite the sin of usury, bishops and kings colluded to allow Jews to lend money, but not to engage in any other form of commerce or trade—thus offloading the sin of usury on them.

How Long Did They Take to Build?

The average construction time was between 250 and 300 years. A major variable was the availability of funding. The main body of Salisbury took only 46 years to complete, and about 100 years overall. Westminster Abbey took 75 years. Since Westminster had royal patronage, funding was more reliable, plus the king could impress laborers. By contrast, Canterbury Cathedral took 343 years.

Map of church locations

PART TWO

Profiles of Selected Gothic Cathedrals and Churches

Selection Criteria

England is full of marvelous Gothic religious buildings of all kinds. Each is interesting in its own way. To make our selection for this guidebook, we applied several filters. They are: unique architectural attributes; buildings which help showcase the evolution of the Gothic style from the Early Gothic to the Perpendicular; historical importance; and geographical diversity. We also attempted to guess which finite number of Gothic churches would be of the greatest interest and accessibility for potential visitors. Finally, as a practical matter, we were obligated to place an upper limit on the number that could be included, and thus were forced to leave out many exceptional buildings.

In the end, the following 11 cathedrals, one abbey, and one chapel are included in this book: The cathedrals are Canterbury, Durham, Ely, Exeter, Gloucester, Lincoln, Peterborough, Salisbury, Wells, Winchester, and York. Plus, Westminster Abbey and King's College Chapel. They are grouped according to their respective official administrative regions: London and south east, east, northeast, and southwest.

Church Orientation

Medieval churches are usually built on an East-West axis. Hence, the front facade of the church is on the west, and the most sacred area is on the east. This is a key guidepost since important architectural or historical features of a church listed in this book are described using directional terms like east and south. Facing the west front, the south side is on the right, while the left is the north side.

In order to make it easier for visitors to follow, each church profile includes a floor plan with a suggested visit sequence. The number on each "stop" during a visit corresponds to the organization of the text.

PROFILES OF THE 13 CHURCHES

LONDON AND SOUTHEAST

Cloister, Canterbury

Westminster Abbey

Personal Impressions

All great medieval churches are historically and architecturally complex. Of the many we have visited and studied in England, Westminster Abbey is the hardest to describe. Both a museum and a church, its vast space is a warren of memorials, tombs, and shrines. In addition to its fascinating history, the abbey has some of the most interesting, sometimes sublime, architecture and aesthetics of any Gothic church.

Approximately two million visitors a year are drawn to this famous, beautiful, fundamental part of English history. It is hard to grasp the enormity of the structure from the outside, given its setting in the midst of urban London. From the outside, the abbey is not that impressive. In fact, the nearby Parliament building may seem much more regal, attractive, and sumptuous. We wondered why so many people were willing to wait so long, and pay so much, to visit this building. Then, we learned.

North side view

While the abbey has a simple yet majestic west front, the highlight of the exterior is the façade of the north transept. It is full of more architectural and decorative features than any other transept façade among the English Gothic churches: a lovely carved tympanum (the triangular area on a façade at the top of a portal), rose window, gables, and extravagant buttresses.

The beauty and size of the interior created a feeling of excitement, which continued until we exited many hours later full of awe at this human and spiritual masterpiece. The abbey, built largely by Henry III from 1245, is not just a place for prayer—it is indeed a paragon of architecture, power, religion, politics, finance, art, and literature.

Our favorite parts of the interior are Poet's Corner and the Tudor-Stuart tombs. Poets' Corner touched us deeply, just looking at those familiar names of England's literary greats: Kipling, the Brontë sisters, Robert and Elizabeth Browning, Lord Byron, Chaucer, Dickens, T.S. Eliot, Hardy, Oscar Wilde, and Shakespeare of course. Their names, engraved in stones on the floor, on the walls, and on their tombs, were indescribably moving. Although this part of the abbey doesn't have any remarkable architectural beauty or religious symbolism, it was significant to us.

Outshining all else, however, is the Henry VII Lady Chapel; for us, the most magical space in England, maybe all of Europe. This is a church one has to visit more than once to grasp its historical and architectural complexity. Westminster Abbey is so much more than just a religious structure.

History

Around 970 CE, Benedictine monks built an abbey on this site. In about 1052 Edward the Confessor rebuilt the abbey to provide himself with a royal burial place. The incomplete building was consecrated in late 1065, only a week before his death. The first church in England built in the Norman style, it became known as the "west minster" to distinguish it from the earlier St Paul's Cathedral.

Edward's abbey survived for two centuries until the middle of the 13th century, when Henry III decided to rebuild it in the new Gothic style. It was a great age for churches: France saw the construction of Amiens, Evreux, and Chartres, while England erected Canterbury, Winchester, and Salisbury, to mention a few. Henry's plan physically linked his palace residence with the abbey as his private monastery.

Edward the Confessor's coffin was damaged in the Reformation and was replaced by a simple box on top of the original 13th-century pedestal, which was made of dark Purbeck marble (which is actually not a marble) and inlaid with precious stones. Henry VIII's control over the abbey helped protect it from the destruction which he inflicted on most English abbeys. After that, the status of the abbey ping-ponged across a series of designations. For example, in 1559 Protestant Queen Elizabeth I took control of the religious houses, which had been revived by Catholic Queen Mary, and removed the monks. Then, in 1560 Elizabeth I re-designated the abbey as a so-called 'Royal Peculiar,' i.e., a church responsible directly to the sovereign. The abbey did, however, suffer damage during the turbulent Civil War, when it was attacked by Puritan iconoclasts. It was again protected by its close ties to the Crown.

Since the first documented coronation of William the Conqueror, Westminster Abbey has continued to be the coronation site of almost every British monarch. In 1966 the abbey celebrated its 900th anniversary.

Building

It is difficult for a visitor to grasp what the entire building looks like from the outside, or even from the inside. The interior is especially mystifying. While the west end interior is architecturally rather straightforward, the eastern part, including the transept, is a confusing maze of rooms, monuments, and memorials, many placed one above the other.

Unlike most other Gothic church layouts, the choir is located in the nave before the crossing. The east and west ends are about the same length, not counting the very wide single set of transept arms. The abbey has a rounded, apsidal east end, unusual in English Gothic churches.

Although the abbey's design was influenced by the "French style," English taste dominates as shown in the use of detailed and rich surfaces, tracery, heraldic shields, large-scale sculpted figures, and smaller foliage carvings. But, surely, England's major contribution to Gothic design was its elaborately ribbed and vaulted ceilings. The Henry VII Lady Chapel at Westminster Abbey has one of the greatest of all English fan-vaulted ceilings.

Little remains of the original medieval stained-glass windows, once one of the abbey's chief glories. For example, the great west window and the rose window in the north transept date from the early-18th century, and the remainder of the glass dates from the 19th century onwards.

Virtually all English Gothic churches are used as monuments of the "great and the good." Surely, however, Westminster Abbey is the extreme example of this practice. The abbey serves as the national mausoleum, and it is impossible to discuss any part of the interior without noting some among the memorials to those buried or commemorated there. The place is just packed with 450 tombs, statues, monuments, effigies, plaques, and every sort of memorabilia. Fortunately, many are of interest.

Exterior

WEST FRONT

The overall design of the west front is dominated by the two 18th-century square towers, each of which is exceptionally tall at 225 feet (68m). Squeezed between them at the top is a gable with a tower-mounted clock on each side. Below is the large, pointed west window. The bottom tier is covered with statuary. Above the portal is a frieze of 10 large statues depicting 20th-century martyrs from all over the world. On each side of the portal are two more friezes: four statues representing Truth and Justice on the left; Mercy and Peace on the right.

NORTH TRANSEPT

The entrance to the abbey is via the north transept portal whose façade is huge, imposing, and complex. Four large attached buttresses sustain it, and near the top are two sets of flying buttresses that support the large rose window. Each buttress has a pointed cap. This must be one of the most heavily buttressed façades in English medieval architecture. The builders weren't taking any chances! Other features:

- It has six lancet windows at mid-level, as well as three portals topped with tall pointed gables.
- The large center portal is further decorated with an unusual, and exceptionally fine, tympanum with its statue of Mary and Jesus above the two doors.

- At the top of the tympanum is a seated Jesus flanked by angels. The lintel below depicts the 12 apostles. The lowest tier has figures representing Art, History, Philosophy, War, Legislation, and Science, plus the builders of the abbey, Edward the Confessor, Henry III, and Richard II.

EAST END

The east end is rounded, unlike most English Gothic churches. An exercise in exuberant design, it reminded us of Victorian-era Gothic Revival. It looks quite different from the earlier Gothic designs found in most of the rest of the abbey.

East end

TOWERS

The abbey's two western towers were left unfinished until 1722. The stubby central lantern tower is hardly visible from ground level. This abbreviated structure was built in 1958 to repair World War II damage. The smallish side windows in this lantern tower form the top of the crossing.

BELLS

Following a recent overhaul, the abbey's 10 bells are set up for change ringing. The tenor bell weighs 3,403 lbs (1,544 kilos). In addition there are two bells, cast in 1585 and 1598 respectively, plus a bell cast in 1738.

BUTTRESSES

The abbey is heavily buttressed everywhere one looks. For example, note the proliferation of the large buttresses supporting the side walls. They are attached to the walls seemingly every few feet, with flying buttresses springing inward to fortify the clerestory level. The exuberant lattice-work filled flying buttresses at the top of the rounded east end are notable.

Interior

Given the large number of visitors, the walking route through the abbey has been regulated to manage the flow. The descriptions of the interior sections provided here follow the walkway routes set out by the authorities.

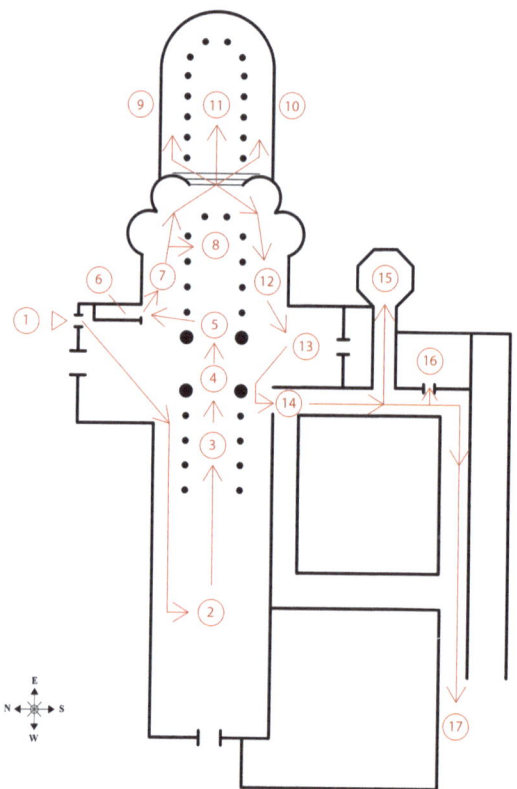

Floor Plan

1. North transept
2. Nave
3. Choir area
4. Crossing
5. High altar area
6. Chapel of Three Saints
7. North ambulatory
8. Edward Confessor platform
9. Queen Elizabeth chapel
10. Queen Mary chapel
11. Henry VII Lady Chapel
12. South ambulatory
13. South transept
14. Cloister
15. Chapter house
16. Pyx chamber
17. Exit

➤ *Visitors enter via the door in the north transept façade [Floor Plan #1].*

NORTH TRANSEPT

The principal foci here are the rose window and the beautiful vaulting on the high ceiling.

➤ *Turn right into the nave [Floor Plan #2].*

NAVE

The nave is narrow and, at 102 feet (31m), has the highest ceiling of any medieval church in England. Most of the nave was built during the last half of the 14th and early-15th centuries. Clustered Purbeck piers with modest capitals line the nave, which is lit by Waterford crystal chandeliers, a gift from the Guinness family for the abbey's 900th anniversary. The nave has 12 arcaded bays with simple traceried windows in each. The north wall of the nave is lined with monuments, including those to Isaac Newton and Charles Darwin. This history of celebrity interment is ongoing. In 2018, they were joined by Stephen Hawking.

Like nearly all major English churches, the abbey has a three-level elevation with pointed arcade arches that rise at least two-thirds of the way to the ceiling. This results in a small windowless triforium and a clerestory.

Ceiling The complex and beautifully vaulted ceiling has ribs which spring from the rising shafts, then fan out to connect with the gilded and bossed ridge rib (a rib which runs down the apex of the vault in a longitudinal direction). The aisle has simple rib vaulting, but is nicely embellished with a cluster of shafts which rise from the upper window level, then veer inward to connect with the ribs.

Nave looking east and choir screen

West End The stained glass in the west window was installed in 1735. The design shows Abraham, Isaac, Jacob, and 14 prophets. At the base are miscellaneous coats of arms, including Elizabeth I, George II, a Dean, and the City of Westminster.

Towards the west front doorway, note the Grave of the Unknown Warrior and the Coronation Chair set in a chapel on the south side. The wooden Coronation Chair has traditionally housed the so-called 'Stone of Scone.' The stone was taken in Scotland in 1296 by Edward I as a spoil of war and moved to Westminster Abbey. Most subsequent English sovereigns have been crowned in this chair. The stone was recently returned to Scotland and will remain alongside the crown jewels of Scotland in Edinburgh until needed for another British coronation.

➢ *Enter the choir area [Floor Plan #3].*

CHOIR AREA

Choir Screen The 18th-century choir screen is a heavily decorated, gilt-covered neo-Gothic work about 25 feet (8m) high. We think it rather too flamboyant.

In the center is a peaked gable covered with several layers of Gothic designs. Each side has a series of white stone statues. The ceiling inside the passageway into the choir is beautifully vaulted, gilded, and painted blue.

Choir Stalls The stalls, made of beautifully carved dark wood, are actually just benches with no misericords (the ledge projecting from the underside of a hinged seat in a choir stall). The walls behind the stalls are a forest of spiky Gothic pinnacles and piers. The stall backs are lined with blue cloth, and the area is lit with stand lights attached to the stalls.

Organ This instrument was built in 1937 and was used for the first time at the coronation of George VI. The two late-19th-century organ cases were re-installed in 1959. The organ was enlarged twice in the 1980s.

➢ *Proceed to the crossing [Floor Plan #4].*

CROSSING

Above the square-shaped crossing is the wonderful ceiling painted with an overall mosaic pattern. On each side are four spiked roundels, which are connected by a four-pointed "star" shape in the center.

➢ *Continue to the high altar area [Floor Plan #5].*

HIGH ALTAR AREA

This is where England's kings and queens are crowned in an elaborate, ancient ceremony. The high altar sits here partially under the crossing. Behind the altar is the jewel-studded alabaster and cedar-wood high altar screen. Both altar and screen were designed by the eminent church restorer, Sir George Gilbert Scott, in 1867. The flamboyantly decorated high altar screen consists of three wide panels. In the center panel is a depiction of the Last Supper. On each side are blind lancet designs under spiky canopies. Four large statues of Moses, St Peter, St Paul, and King David flank the altar and the doors leading into Shrine of Edward the Confessor, which is on a platform immediately behind the screen. In front of the high altar is another of the abbey's treasures: the marble pavement dating from 1268.

➢ *Turn left toward the chapel walled off from the north transept [Floor Plan #6].*

CHAPEL OF THREE SAINTS

This long chapel—devoted to three saints: Andrew, Michael, and John—consists of a maze of monuments of all shapes and sizes. Much of the carving is of a high order. It would be hard to imagine how one could pack any more large sculptures and monuments into this rather small space.

➢ *Proceed to the north ambulatory [Floor Plan #7].*

NORTH AMBULATORY

On the left wall of the ambulatory, visitors pass a series of chapels, filled with monuments and tombs of English worthies. Among them, St John the Baptist's chapel and St Paul's chapel have many fine Elizabethan monuments, including the tallest monument in the abbey at 36 feet (11m) to the first Baron Hunsdon. The wall on the right side, below the platform, contains the tombs of Edward I, Henry III, and Eleanor of Castile.

➢ *Go up the stairs to the Edward the Confessor Platform [Floor Plan #8].*

EDWARD THE CONFESSOR PLATFORM

The platform on the right side of the ambulatory is occupied by the Shrine of Edward the Confessor, which was originally decorated with gold and gems looted by the agents of Henry VIII. At the east end of the platform is the elaborate tomb of Henry V with his queen, Katherine de Valois. Henry V's tomb area is notable for the ornate chapel built above his tomb with two turret staircases leading to the altar above. The platform is not normally accessible to visitors.

➢ *Return to the north ambulatory and proceed to the stairs where the north arm of the ambulatory converges with the south arm. Take the left stairway to the Elizabeth I chapel [Floor Plan #9].*

Shrine of Edward the Confessor

WESTMINSTER ABBEY

ELIZABETH I CHAPEL

On the way to the chapel, note the stairway's handsome barrel-vaulted ceiling with gilded, geometric decorations, painted red and blue.

This narrow and well-lit chapel contains the tombs of Elizabeth I and her Catholic sister Queen Mary Tudor. Elizabeth's tomb is positioned immediately above Mary's—dominance in death as in life?

Elizabeth I tomb

➢ *Return to the stairway landing and up the right-side stairs to the Mary Queen of Scots Chapel [Floor Plan #10].*

MARY QUEEN OF SCOTS CHAPEL

The beheaded body of Mary Queen of Scots was brought here by her son, James I, from Peterborough Cathedral. Surrounded by other tombs and monuments, it seems crowded.

➢ *Return to stair landing and go up the stairs to the Henry VII Lady Chapel [Floor Plan #11].*

HENRY VII LADY CHAPEL

This chapel was constructed by Henry VII at enormous cost in the early-16th century, replacing a 13th-century chapel. The main monument is Henry VII's tomb. The flamboyant Italian Renaissance architecture here is different from that in any other part of the abbey. Lining the north and south walls are handsome dark wood stalls with a tall screen behind. Beneath the hinged seats of the stalls are beautifully carved misericords. The screen is decorated with the coats of arms of knights awarded the Most Honorable Order of the Bath. The banners of the current Knights Grand Cross surround the walls, and above each stall are their respective helms and swords. The chapel's walls are covered with over 100 statues of saints and kings, in addition to the Tudor emblems of rose and portcullis. The upper walls are filled with late Gothic windows,

Henry VII Lady Chapel

supported by thin piers. But the glory of this magical space is the spectacular carved and fan-vaulted ceiling with hanging decorative pendants.

ROYAL AIR FORCE–CROMWELL CHAPEL

The chapel at the end of the rounded apse is dedicated to the Royal Air Force. On the floor is a stone plaque dedicated to Oliver Cromwell—aka The Great Protector. This plaque marks the spot where he was buried with state honors, only to have his body dug up, hung, and decapitated about a year later. The stained-glass east windows are modern.

➢ *Take the stairs into the south ambulatory [Floor Plan #12].*

SOUTH AMBULATORY

Descending the stairway, one passes the St Nicholas and St Edmund chapels, then the chapel of St Benedict, as well as the tombs of Edward III and Richard II with his queen, Anne of Bohemia.

➢ *Proceed to the south transept area [Floor Plan #13].*

SOUTH TRANSEPT

The highlights here include the rose window, which sits above four tiers of arcading. The glass dates only from 1902. Beneath it, in the angles above the right and left arches, are two medieval carvings depicting angels. Note the two fine late-13th-century wall paintings, uncovered in 1936, to be seen by the door leading to St Faith chapel. Legend has it that the chapel door was once covered with the skins of Danes.

The major draw for many in this area is the Poet's Corner, which was not originally designated as the burial place of writers, playwrights, and poets. The first poet to be buried here was Geoffrey Chaucer, so honored because he had been Clerk of Works to the Palace of Westminster, not because he had written the *Canterbury Tales*.

➢ *Reenter the nave and take the first doorway on the left into the cloister [Floor Plan #14].*

Poet's Corner

CLOISTER

The cloister is filled with old and new monuments. Each of the four cloister walkways is approximately 100 feet (30m) in length, dating mainly from the 13th to the 15th centuries. The ceiling is a simple ribbed design, and the cloister windows are decorated with abundant tracery.

➢ *Proceed to the chapter house [Floor Plan #15].*

CHAPTER HOUSE

This octagonal chapter house is said to be one of the finest and largest in England. It was built by Henry III in 1250, then restored in the late 19th century. The entrance is via the east cloister walkway, through a double doorway with a large tympanum above. The doorway is decorated with sculptured figures in the moldings. In the center of the room is a slender, clustered pillar from which the vaulting springs. This vault is a restoration. The walls have the remains of 14th-century paintings and numerous stone benches above which are large and innovative quatrefoil windows. The original 13th-century windows were "lost" by the 18th century, while the remainder were destroyed in World War II. The mid-13th century tiled pavement is original. A door within the chapter house vestibule dates from around 1050, and is believed to be the oldest in England. The exterior includes flying buttresses added in the 14th century and a leaded roof with a lantern tower. Its many historical functions have included its use as a daily meeting place in the 13th century for Benedictine monks, and as a meeting place of the King's Great Council and the Commons, which preceded the Parliament.

Chapter house

➢ *Turn left and enter the Pyx chapel [Floor Plan #16].*

PYX CHAPEL

This late-11th-century Norman chapel was the underground monks' dormitory, also used as a treasury. The term "pyx" refers to the boxwood chest in which coins were held. Newly minted coins were presented at the Trial of the Pyx to ensure they conformed to the required standards.

➢ *Proceed to the exit [Floor Plan #17].*

QUEEN'S DIAMOND JUBILEE GALLERIES

These new galleries, opened in mid-June 2018, are located in the medieval triforium. On display are the 300 or so greatest treasures from the abbey's collection, which tell the story of its 1,000-year history. Visitors reach the Jubilee Galleries through a new tower, housing a staircase and lift. Named the Weston Tower, this first major addition to the abbey since 1745 offers previously unseen views of the Palace of Westminster. The tower is located between the abbey's chapter house and Lady Chapel.

Canterbury Cathedral

Three-quarter view

Personal Impressions

We took the short train ride from London to Canterbury and walked to our hotel near the cathedral. The ancient cathedral town of Canterbury is small, walkable, and charming. While maintaining its antique charm, it has adapted to today's world in a nice way. For example, the many Asian restaurants set in ancient buildings amidst quintessential pubs and quaint bookstores looked as though they had been there forever. There were no high-rises and no traffic lights in the main street. Students of all races dressed in school uniforms mingled around after school. The whole area felt welcoming.

In the middle of the tiny town center, we almost missed the entrance to the cathedral. Canterbury Cathedral is not easily visible from the street as it is set behind a gated structure—itself an interesting one—and commercial buildings.

Passing through the stone gate, one leaves behind the throngs of tourists and locals to find an oasis of calm. A large grassy compound is dotted with trees which provided a lovely setting. Although getting a good look at the front of the cathedral was hard, as it is hemmed in with houses and commercial buildings, the three-quarter view of the front and south side is fine.

Old stone gate

The cathedral is filled with many wonders. Of particular note are the beautiful vaulted ceilings in the chapter house and in the cloister. The most impressive feature is, however, the tangible "presence" of St Thomas Becket. This was especially felt at the spot where he was murdered, by the lonely candle in Trinity Chapel where his tomb had been, and by his visage looking down from ancient stained glass windows. We were told that devoted pilgrims still make their way here on foot. But surely no one does this as dramatically as Henry II, who entered the city in 1174 on bare, bloodied feet to seek atonement for his role in the murder of St Thomas.

Outside the cathedral walking through the remnants of Canterbury's monastic past, we felt immersed in history.

History

The local Anglo-Saxon king in Kent offered a church to Abbot Augustine to use as a place of worship. It is said that the king was married to a Christian who influenced him to initiate the restoration of this church, believed to be the current St Martin's. Dating to Roman times, it is the oldest church in England still in use. Augustine built the first cathedral nearby, becoming the first Archbishop of Canterbury. Until the 10th century, the cathedral community was part of the household of the Archbishop. During the 10th century the Benedictines established their separate community, which continued until the monastery was dissolved by Henry VIII in 1540.

The early cathedral was destroyed by fire in 1067, a year after the Norman Conquest. Rebuilding was based largely on the design of the abbey of St Etienne in Caen, France. It was dedicated in 1077. In 1096, the east end was replaced with a 198-foot extension, which doubled the length of the cathedral. The addition was set above the large and elaborately decorated crypt.

In 1170, Henry II's knights murdered Archbishop Thomas Becket in the northwest transept, the area now called The Martyrdom. He became an instant martyr and a saint, which made this cathedral especially attractive to pilgrims. There is now a stunning contemporary "swords sculpture" memorializing the murder.

The choir was severely damaged by fire in 1174, necessitating a major reconstruction. The master-mason appointed to rebuild the choir was a Frenchman, William of Sens. His design of the new choir signaled a major shift to the Gothic style in England—aka The French style. This marked a decisive, influential moment in English church architecture. The choir was back in use by 1180. Other architectural features were replaced in the new Gothic style, with pointed arches, ribbed vaulting, and flying buttresses. In place of the old, square-ended, eastern chapel, the present Trinity and Corona chapels were constructed to house Thomas' shrine. Another major reason for this renovation was to accommodate the flood of pilgrims visiting his shrine.

The cathedral was seriously damaged by an earthquake in 1382, causing the loss of its bells and free-standing tower. This resulted in many more renovation and "updating" projects throughout the cathedral. These include the 1505 fan-vaulted ceiling in the crossing and the tomb of the Black Prince.

Renovation efforts among England's churches over the years were a mix of good work and bad by generations of clergy and public aesthetes. Here at Canterbury, for example, in 1790 the entire interior was crudely coated with whitewash.

The formal break with Rome during the Reformation prompted the destruction of the magnificent shrine of Becket in 1538, by order of Henry VIII. Many other costly shrines shared its fate. The king accused the dead Becket of being a traitor. All the tomb's gold and jewels were taken and Thomas's bones were burnt. There was so much loot it took 26 carts to haul it away. One of the jewels, a large ruby given by the king of France, is now part of the crown jewels in the Tower of London. As outlandish as it seems, Henry directed the dead saint to appear at court to face charges of treason. Since Becket did not appear, he was found guilty. The monastic part of the cathedral was dissolved in 1539.

Then, during the Civil War, the Puritans broke much of the medieval glass; toppled altars; stripped lead from the roof; defaced or broke brasses and effigies; and stabled horses in the nave. By the end of this destructive orgy little was left but bare walls and masses of broken fragments.

During World War II, the cathedral's beautiful stained-glass windows were removed for safekeeping from German air raids, then put back after the war. These temporary windows were destroyed by German bombs. A large part of Canterbury town was also destroyed, as was the cathedral library, but the main body of the cathedral remained intact.

Canterbury Cathedral is the Mother Church of the worldwide Anglican Communion. It is the seat of the Archbishop of Canterbury, who is the symbolic head of the Communion and the principal leader of the Church of England. The Church of England is divided into two provinces, with the Archbishop of Canterbury leading the southern province, while the Archbishop of York leads the northern one.

Building

Canterbury is 525 feet (160m) long overall, due mainly to the eastern "arm." Only Winchester and Ely cathedrals are longer. The nave, western transepts, and central tower are fine examples of the Perpendicular style.

The cathedral has a double cruciform floor plan, with its two sets of transepts. The east end has a rounded apse in the French tradition. Since it was originally an abbey, Canterbury has a cloister and a chapter house.

The interior layout is unusual: It is stepped, rising dramatically from the west to the east. The choir is higher than the nave, and from there one mounts steps to the high altar area, the Trinity Chapel, and on up to the Corona Chapel at the east end.

Exterior

WEST FRONT

The west front is dominated by its two large, decorated towers, by its huge multi-paneled window, and by the two massive, attached buttresses supporting each tower.

TOWERS AND BELLS

The cathedral has three towers: the two on the west front and the third at the crossing. Each western tower is 130 feet (40m) high. Note the prominent pinnacles at the top of each corner of all three towers. The cathedral has a total of 21 bells in its three towers.

Southwest Tower This tower on the right side is known as the Oxford Tower. The original southwest tower was replaced in 1458 with the present one in the Perpendicular style. This tower contains the cathedral's main set of 14 bells, cast only in 1981. The heaviest bell here is the so-called 'Great Dunston Bell,' which weighs 6,200 lbs (2,812 kilos). It tolls the hours.

Northwest Tower The tower on the left is also known as the Arundel Tower. The original Norman-style tower was replaced in 1834 with this Perpendicular-style twin of the other west front tower. This was the last major structural alteration to the cathedral. This tower contains the cathedral's chiming clock.

Central Lantern Tower Also called the Bell Harry Tower, this tower is 236 feet (72m) high. The present tower was begun in 1433, then strengthened in the early-16th century. It has tall, pointed windows on two levels. Overall, this is an unusually handsome tower. The oldest bell in the cathedral is the "Bell Harry," which hangs in a cage atop this tower and is the basis of the tower's name. This bell was cast in 1635. It tolls at 8 a.m. and 9 p.m. daily to announce the opening and closing of the cathedral, and also tolls occasionally for services.

SOUTH SIDE

The side and rear three-quarter views of the exterior of Canterbury Cathedral reveal its great size and complexity.

Southwest Porch This mid-15th-century southwest porch is the main entrance to the cathedral. Note the sculpture-filled niches surrounding the porch, which juts out from the south wall below the southwest tower. In the mid-19th century, these formerly vacant niches of the cathedral were filled with statues of historic personages connected with the province or with the history of the church.

Buttresses and Projections The nave walls are supported by large buttress piers set between each arcade window. Just above these windows, note the small vestigial triforium window openings. At the clerestory level, the buttress piers support another line of buttresses which intersect the wall between each clerestory window. Further east are the south transept façade and St Anselm's chapel, both of which project far from the choir wall.

EAST END

The rounded eastern end has windows on three levels: crypt, Trinity Chapel, and clerestory. The apse walls are supported by large attached buttresses set between the windows.

MONASTIC BUILDINGS

These buildings were separate from the areas managed by secular clergy, such as the stables, granaries, barn, bake house, brew house, and laundry. Far from the cathedral stood other buildings dedicated to the relief of the poor, which included a pauper's hospice and a great hall. Near the common room of the

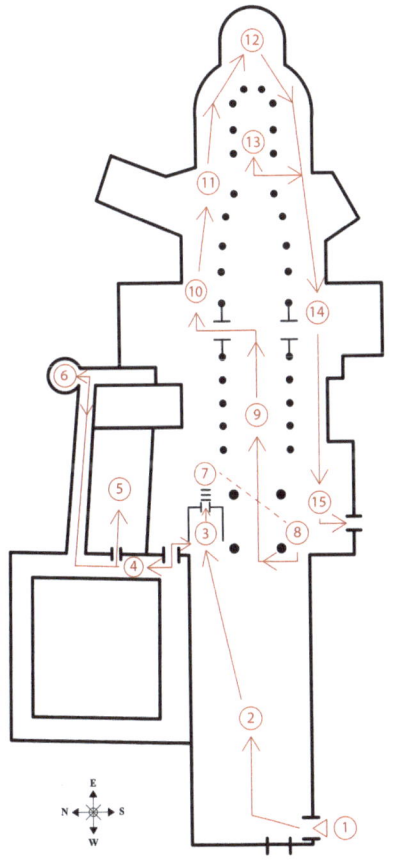

Floor Plan

1. Southwest portal
2. Nave
3. Northwest transept
4. Cloister
5. Chapter house
6. Water tower
7. Crypt entrance
8. Crypt exit
9. Choir area
10. North choir aisle
11. Ambulatory
12. Corona chapel
13. Trinity chapel
14. South choir aisle
15. Southwest transept and exit

monks was a "lavatory" building in the form of a Norman hall, 145 feet (44m) long by 25 feet (8m) wide, with 55 seats. It was hygienic, with a stream of water running through it.

Interior

➢ *Enter through the southwest portal [Floor Plan #1], and proceed to the nave [Floor Plan #2].*

Nave looking east

NAVE

The Norman nave and transepts survived until the late-14th century, when they were demolished to make way for the present Perpendicular architecture.

Elevation The nave elevation has the usual three levels: arcade, triforium, and clerestory. The tall nave arcade left the clerestories small, and the triforium is now little more than an unglazed extension of the clerestory. Most light comes from the tall arcade windows, which gives the interior a feeling of space. The piers which support the nave are slim and handsome; the horizontal lines give way to the vertical; and the shafts soar from the floor to the vault. For the first time in England, dark Purbeck marble was used for the shafts, which established the tradition.

Ceiling The nave ceiling is 80 feet (24m) high. The nave vaults are a grand network of complex ribbing, with a six-sided figure at the apex, where the flaring ribs join from the wall-mounted shafts.

Pulpit On the north side of the nave is the pulpit, a fine confection of colored carvings and a tall canopy. Note the elegant pulpit stairs, topped with sculptured figures. It is attached to one of the piers on the north side of the nave.

West Window This window was originally installed in the late-12th century. The current window is made up of fragments of old glass. One of the most notable panels is the depiction of Adam in the bottom row, fourth from right—often called the Adam delving (or digging). This genealogy (aka Tree of Jesse) window features depictions of 13 of Christ's ancestors.

Font The 1637 black and white marble font is in the north nave aisle. The Rococo cover is highly decorated with figures of the four Evangelists and other Apostles.

Adam delving panel

➢ *Proceed to the northwest transept [Floor Plan #3].*

NORTHWEST TRANSEPT
(AKA THE MARTYRDOM TRANSEPT)

The northwest transept is down a stairway from the crossing. The landing here is also called The Martyrdom, as this is the alleged site of Becket's murder. Behind the simple altar is a fine modern sculpture. Overlooking it is the chantry of an archbishop. Next door is the Lady Chapel with its two forgettable 17th-century monuments. Note the great royal window showing Edward IV, his daughter, and the two tragic princes murdered in the Tower of London.

➢ *From here pass through the large wooden doors to the cloister [Floor Plan #4].*

Becket sculpture

CLOISTER, CHAPTER HOUSE, AND WATER TOWER

Cloister Adjoining the cathedral on the north side is the 14th-century cloister which was later repaired and complex vaulting added. The vaults which decorate the ceilings are exceptionally beautiful, the ribs decorated with heraldic bosses.

Cloister

➤ *Enter the chapter house via the east walkway of the cloister [Floor Plan #5].*

Chapter House The 11th-century rectangular chapter house is the largest in England. It has a remarkable so-called barrel-vaulted ceiling, made from Irish oak. Its two large, handsome windows are late Victorian.

➤ *Take the passageway to the water tower [Floor Plan #6].*

Water Tower A passage east of the cloister and the chapter house leads to the 12th-century water tower, which was the source of the water supply. The upper part houses a cistern supported by carved Norman piers. The old cloister, now only a partially walled grassy area, is just outside.

➤ *Return to the northwest transept and go down the stairway into the crypt [Floor Plan # 7].*

Barrel-vaulted ceiling

CRYPT

The massive crypt beneath the east end of the cathedral is a "must visit." Built in the early 1100s, it has extensive murals, many carved piers and capitals, and several ancient chapels. A modern, suspended wire sculpture by Antony Gormley is also noteworthy.

➢ *Exit the crypt on the south side and turn right to the crossing platform [Floor Plan #8].*

CROSSING

Above the crossing is the spectacular fan-vaulted ceiling of the tower. The ceiling is set above two rows of blind arched

Crypt chapel

openings. Above these are two windows on each of the four sides of the lantern tower which provide illumination. The ceiling consists of eight semi- and quarter-circles of ribs which swirl around high above.

When the Bell Harry central lantern tower was rebuilt to stabilize it in the early-16th century, large stone braces were added between the huge crossing piers.

➢ *Enter the choir area [Floor Plan #9].*

CHOIR AND HIGH ALTAR AREAS

Choir Screen The nave terminates at the stone choir screen at the back of the crossing platform. The screen was built about 1455. In the Middle Ages this screen had been painted in vivid colors and had statues of the 12 apostles. The early screen was largely destroyed during the Civil War. Only the statues of the shield-bearing angels and six kings survive today. The statues of the kings are all representations of the House of Lancaster, a bias also seen at York Minster.

Organ This must be one of the most peculiar organ layouts in any English Gothic church. The organ console is located on top of the choir screen, out of sight. Also out of sight are the main organ pipes, which are located in the south triforium above the choir area. To make things more complex, a supplementary set of pipes was installed in the north nave aisle in a window opening! Practically all of this equipment dates only from the late 1970s to the early 1980s.

Choir Stalls and High Altar Area The choir stalls have only two rows. At the back of the stalls on each side, a handsome wall of carved stone separates the choir from the side aisles. In the late-17th century, the 13th-century misericords were replaced on each side of the choir. When George Scott carried out renovations in the 19th century, he replaced the front row of these misericords. These Victorian replacements appear to include copies of those in other churches. Note the extravagant Archbishop's Throne at the east end of the choir stalls. Past the choir area, up a flight of steps, is the high altar. There is no altar screen, which permits an unrestricted view of the rounded east end.

➢ *Exit the choir area and turn into the north choir aisle [Floor Plan #10].*

NORTH CHOIR AISLE

This aisle is lined with chantries, murals, and windows. The Chichele Tomb, at the exit from the choir–high altar area, is one of the finest in the cathedral. The colorful carved and painted "archway" surrounds the fine effigy of the 15th-century bishop. As often done during the Middle Ages, below the effigy is one of his gaunt cadaver-to-be. Just to the left, two fascinating "Bible study" windows survive. They date from about 1180 and are thus older than the Becket windows in the ambulatory. There were originally six of these windows but they were later reconfigured into two. The surviving late-12th and early-13th-century glass may be the finest in England.

NORTHEAST TRANSEPT

The main item of interest in the northeast transept is the Victorian clock. It has a mother-of-pearl face with Roman numerals. The long pendulum has a bob at the end picturing a sunburst surrounding a face. Beyond this transept, note the painted ceiling of the Norman chapel.

➢ *Continue into the ambulatory area [Floor Plan #12].*

AMBULATORY

The ambulatory begins at the top of the stairs and runs around the outside of the Trinity Chapel.

Becket Windows The north aisle has some of the cathedral's most important stained glass. The majority is original from about 1180 to 1220, although significant restorations (and replacements) were made in the 19th century. At the top of the steps in the first window of the ambulatory is the famous image of St Thomas in his archbishop robes, giving a blessing. It is modern but made from old glass.

Above this window is another showing Becket holding his primate's cross. All around are the vivid 13th-century windows, illustrating Becket's miracles. The rest tell stories of ordinary people who experienced miracles by praying to him or visiting his shrine. These narratives provide a fascinating glimpse into medieval life, particularly illnesses and accidents.

St Thomas Becket panel

Tomb of Henry IV and Joan of Navarre Further along the ambulatory is the important tomb of Henry IV and his wife, Joan of Navarre.

➢ *Continue clockwise around the ambulatory to the Corona Chapel [Floor Plan #12].*

Corona Chapel This chapel, also known as "Crown Chapel," is located in an extension of the apse. It was added to the Trinity Chapel to house a few Becket relics and some fine windows. The relics are said to include the top of his skull—his corona—struck off during his assassination. The chapel features two medieval windows of interest, both of which date from about 1200: the Tree of Jesse window and the redemption window. Only two bottom panels of the left window are the original Tree of Jesse window: panels showing King Josiah at the top and the Virgin Mary below. The rest of the window has clear glass. The next window to the right is a modern version of the Tree of Jesse window. The redemption window, behind the altar, shows four Old Testament scenes related to the Passion and Resurrection.

Tomb of the Black Prince Another important tomb is that of Edward the Black Prince, an English national hero who fought at Crécy and Poitiers. Above his tomb is a canopy, on top of which are the remains of dress and armor actually worn by him. The Norman–French inscription on the tomb reads: "Here lies the most noble Prince Edward, eldest son of the most noble

King Edward III, Prince of Aquitaine and Wales, Duke of Cornwall and Earl of Chester, who died on Trinity Sunday, the 8th of June 1376. To the soul of whom God grant mercy. Amen."

➢ *Continue clockwise and enter the Trinity Chapel [Floor Plan #13].*

TRINITY CHAPEL

Becket Shrine The Becket shrine had been located at the center of the Trinity Chapel. It sat on a stone base with marble arches and was covered with a wooden canopy. It was embellished with gold and set with pearls and jewels. This space remains the premier religious place in England. This original Becket shrine was destroyed by Henry VIII during the Reformation. Now, instead of a shrine, a simple candle sits in the middle of the floor where the shrine had been. Note how the original floor around the shrine is worn by the knees of innumerable pilgrims. Pilgrim donations paid for much of the subsequent rebuilding of the cathedral and its associated buildings.

St Augustine's Chair At the western edge of the Trinity Chapel is this 13th-century marble chair where England's senior archbishops have been enthroned.

➢ *Exit the Trinity Chapel via the steps into the south choir aisle [Floor Plan #14].*

ST ANSELM'S CHAPEL AND THE SOUTHEAST TRANSEPT

To the left is St Anselm's chapel with a wall painting of St Paul. This chapel projects far out from the south wall. Further down the choir aisle is the southeast transept, which is similar to the northeast. The earliest colored-glass windows are from the late-12th century. The rest are recent, for example, the four Ervin Bossányi windows added only in 1957.

SOUTHWEST TRANSEPT

Genealogy Window This area is the locus of the Genealogy Window on the south wall: the cathedral's first great display of stained glass. It is the widest window in the cathedral at 25 feet (8m) and has a height of 55 feet (17m). Its three tiers of stained-glass panels date from the late-12th to the early-13th centuries. The most important image in this window is Methuselah in the bottom row, fourth panel from right. This window, perhaps the oldest glass in England, was recently restored at great cost.

St Michael Chapel Facing the chapel is the bell from the HMS Canterbury, which is rung to commemorate the military dead. The chapel (aka Warrior's Chapel) is full of military banners and dedications, as is the window on the east wall. In the center is the marvelous tomb with effigies of the 15th-century Lady Margaret Holland with her two husbands.

➢ *Continue to the southwest transept, and exit [Floor Plan #15].*

Winchester Cathedral

Personal Impressions

Part of the pleasure of visiting Winchester Cathedral is approaching it through this ancient city's narrow streets, which give one the feeling of walking into the past. The town is also a treasure house of medieval buildings, each of which is worth a visit. The cathedral is situated in the middle of a large, grassy compound filled with huge trees that prevent a full view of the building.

It is hard to know what to expect from a given cathedral just from reading about it and looking at a few photos—or even when standing in front of it. Of all the cathedrals we have visited, the disconnect between the exterior and the interior may be the most extreme in the case of Winchester Cathedral. The cathedral is known for its sheer massiveness, as well as its truncated central tower. The exterior of the building is surprisingly austere, far from dramatic, in part due to its lack of significant towers.

West front

The inside is a different story. Once inside, we were wowed far more by its aesthetics and many special features than by its size. To name just a few, we marveled at: the overly sumptuous chantries of several bishops; the medieval black marble font heavily carved on all four sides; the Holy Sepulcher chapel with some of the best 12th-century wall paintings in the country; and Jane Austen's tomb.

On the way to find the modest dwelling where Jane Austen lived her final months and died, we chanced upon the largely destroyed Wolvesey Castle. We were unprepared for the surreal beauty and grandeur of it, even in ruins. It was the residence of the Bishops of Winchester since Anglo-Saxon times. The last great occasion here was on 25 July 1554, when Queen Mary Tudor and Philip of Spain held their wedding breakfast in the East Hall. Walking back into town alongside the handsome River Itchen was also a pleasure.

For a history buff, the Great Hall should not be missed. Although created well after King Arthur's time, the large reproduction of the Round Table here is nevertheless referred to as King Arthur's Round Table. It is worth seeing, as is the rare wooden hammer beam (a combination of beams, braces, and rafters that help support a roof's weight) ceiling.

History

Winchester Cathedral has played an exceptionally meaningful role among England's major churches. This is mainly because the town of Winchester was the capital of the most important Anglo-Saxon kingdom, and this cathedral was for a period the major royal church in England.

Work began on the present building soon after the Conquest in 1066, next to the original mid-7th century Anglo-Saxon church. Conversion to the Early Gothic style began with the east end in the late-12th century. A new west front and the conversion of the nave into the Gothic style were not done until the mid-14th century. The nave conversion consisted of heavily re-cladding the Norman piers to give them a "modern" appearance and the addition of the spectacular vaults. Many renovations and replacements were done throughout the cathedral in the 18th, and especially in the 19th, century. The original crypt, transept, and the basic structure of the nave survive today.

The cathedral is the burial site of some of the earliest kings of Wessex, including Alfred the Great and the 9th-century St Swithun. The saint's bones were said to heal the sick, and thousands of pilgrims flocked to the cathedral. Stalls were set up to sell relics and clay models of the parts of the body that required healing. These were then placed in the shrine in the hope of a miracle cure. Among other things, this devotion made the Winchester bishops among the wealthiest people in England, and perhaps in Europe.

Henry VIII dissolved the Winchester monastery in 1539, and demolished St Swithun's shrine, the cloister, and the chapter house. A good deal of additional damage was done by a Protestant bishop. During the Civil War, Cromwell's forces did further damage, deliberately smashing the huge medieval stained-glass west window, among other acts of vandalism.

Building

Winchester Cathedral has the greatest overall length of any intact medieval Gothic cathedral in Europe. The building is a whopping 556 feet (170m) in length, in contrast to the nave height of only 78 feet (24m), and modest tower height of 150 feet (46m). The floor plan of the building is uncomplicated, with only a single transept, no projecting chapels, and with no cloister or chapter house.

The builders chose a site so marshy that thousands of wooden piles had to be driven into the ground to make it solid enough to support this enormous church. Despite this precaution, the foundations have been at risk of collapse for centuries. In the early-20th century the waterlogged foundations were reinforced with 25,000 bags of concrete, 115,000 concrete blocks, and a million bricks. A diver worked every day from 1906 to 1912 in total darkness at depths of up to 20 feet (6m). This effort is credited with saving the cathedral from total collapse, although the crypt still floods from time to time.

Exterior

WEST FRONT

The west front is plain, thanks to its vertical style and lack of statuary or other decoration. There are no towers on the west front, only a tall pyramidal gable and two flanking mini-towers, both topped with pinnacles. A central portal has three doors, and there is also a smaller portal on each side. But the dominant feature of the west end is the huge arched window set in a Gothic stone frame.

TOWER

The original central tower collapsed in 1107. Its replacement, which survives today, is still in the Norman style with rounded arched windows. Given the unstable ground, the present tower is a squat, square structure, which rises only 35 feet (11m) above the ridge of the transept roof. The tower is fitted with a set of bells hung in a full-circle to enable change ringing. Most were cast in 1937, the newer ones only in 1992. The heaviest bell weighs 4,000 lbs (1.8 tons).

BUTTRESSES

The south wall of the exterior has heavy two-level flying buttresses emanating from huge stand-alone piers. But even they support only the wall of the arcade level! From the outside, the nave walls appear to have only two elevations: arcade and clerestory. But that is because the triforium level here is minimal and unglazed. A careful look also reveals that there is a row of flying buttresses on both the north and south sides of the cathedral at the clerestory level above the high altar area.

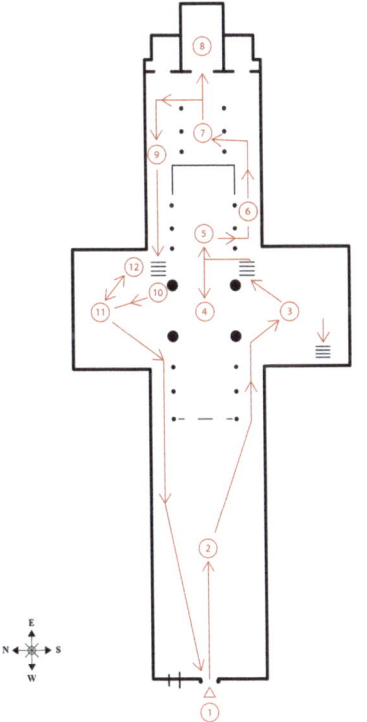

Floor Plan

1. West front
2. Nave
3. South transept
4. Crossing-Choir area
5. High altar area
6. South choir aisle
7. East end
8. Lady Chapel
9. North choir aisle
10. Chapel of Holy Sepulcher
11. North transept
12. Crypt

WINCHESTER CATHEDRAL

Interior

➢ *Enter via the west front [Floor Plan #1] to the nave [Floor Plan #2].*

NAVE

Entering the vast, soaring nave is a wonderful experience, thanks to its scale and fine aesthetics. The light-colored stone provides the nave with good illumination, despite the large, thick piers and lack of a glazed triforium. This nave is based upon the 14th- to 15th-century Perpendicular design, which modified the original Norman piers, walls, and vaulted ceiling. The 14th-century builders transformed the nave by adding new window tracery and by concealing the Norman features. For example, the piers are thick, due to casing the Norman originals with Perpendicular stonework. Do not miss the bronze statues of Charles I and James I on each side of the west door. The stairs up to the treasury are above the entrance area.

Ceiling The dominant feature of the nave—indeed perhaps the cathedral as a whole—is the remarkable vaulting throughout. Here in the nave, the vaulting is steeply pitched, consisting of an elegant blizzard of ribs going in all directions. The main supporting ribs spring from smallish carved-stone corbels, positioned atop single shafts which rise from the floor. The bosses depict three medieval bishops, John of Gaunt, and Richard II. The vaulting over the side aisles is of an older, simpler design.

Nave ceiling

Windows After the cathedral's medieval stained-glass west window was deliberately smashed by Cromwell's forces, its hundreds of pieces were assembled into a mosaic window with no attempt to reconstruct the original images. The windows at the arcade and the clerestory levels are mostly clear glass.

Font The dramatic 12th-century square black marble font sits atop short columns. The marvelous carvings celebrate the life of St Nicholas. One side depicts a ship which commemorates how he saved the lives of those at sea, while another depicts how he miraculously brought three students back to life after they had been murdered. This masterpiece is surely one of England's finest.

Font

Monuments The monuments of interest in the nave are the two chantries on the south aisle. Like all of the chantries at Winchester, these two are elaborate complexes of carved white stone in the spiky late Gothic style. These include:

- Bishop Edingdon's chantry (1345–1366): Its alabaster effigy is one of the cathedral's finest medieval sculptures.
- Bishop Wykeham's chantry: Inside is his effigy with two angels holding the pillow under his head, and three monks at his feet praying for his soul.

Other noteworthy monuments include:
- Crimean War Memorial: There are plaques and monuments to commemorate some heroes of the Crimean War.
- Jane Austen plaque: One of the popular attractions is the discreet floor tomb and brass wall plaque to Jane Austen in the north nave aisle. She died in Winchester in 1817. The inscription on her tombstone makes no mention of her novels, but a later brass tablet describes her as "known to many by her writings."

➢ *Proceed toward south transept [Floor Plan # 3].*

SOUTH TRANSEPT

Note the Norman architecture, the wooden ceiling, and the Bishop Wilberforce memorial. This transept is also the burial place of Izaak Walton: author of *The Compleat Angler*. Stairs lead up to the library and triforium gallery.

➢ *Continue to the crossing–choir area [Floor Plan #4].*

CROSSING

The square vaulted ceiling is an elegant design of four fan-shaped rib designs emanating from each corner. At the center space has a round medallion whose ribs are a dark color against a lighter background. This beautiful ceiling is made entirely of wood.

Crossing ceiling

CHOIR AREA

The choir area begins at the western boundary of the crossing and extends east to the middle of the transepts, on each side. Thus, the crossing ceiling sits directly above most of the choir.

Choir Screen Cromwell's soldiers destroyed an older screen. The current screen separating the nave from the choir is Victorian, but is in the Decorated style. It is tall and spiky, carved from dark wood.

Choir screen and stalls

Stall carvings

Choir Stalls Dating from about 1300, these choir stalls are considered by many to be among the finest in England. They are backed by a towering wall of wood carvings.

Organ This modest, wall-mounted organ plays only a minor visual role in the choir area.

Misericord Carvings These carvings on the benches used by the clergy depict all manner of subjects: human, animal, mythical, and floral, just like those behind the stalls. Every inch, including the spandrels and aisle dividers, is covered with carvings of all sizes—many uncommonly large—including a warrior with a flowing mustache that morphs into a "green man" vine, a falconer, and so much more. Lovely lighting of the stall backs adds to the drama.

Bishop's Throne As is so often the case in English Gothic churches, the grand bishop's throne here is a testament to the power of these top religious officials. Such extravagant designs proliferated in the Middle Ages.

➢ *Proceed to the high altar area [Floor Plan #5].*

HIGH ALTAR AREA

This is an especially handsome area. It has two special features: the early-15h-century Great Screen in carved white stone, and the lovely wooden, multi-ribbed vaulted ceiling, filled with gilded heraldic bosses. Although it would take binoculars to see it clearly, the central boss contains the initial "HR," which refers to Henry VII. The original painted statues which adorned the altar screen's niches were destroyed during the Reformation. The present statues are late 19th-century replacements.

High altar screen

This area is lined on each side with tall stone screens which have six painted Renaissance mortuary chests set on top. Since Cromwell's soldiers scattered the bones of the interred kings, it is impossible to know whose bones are in each chest.

➢ *Exit to the south choir aisle [Floor Plan #6] and proceed to the east end [Floor Plan #7]*

EAST END

The large, open east end spans the entire width of the cathedral. The area includes the Lady Chapel. Nearly all this part was built between 1189 and 1204. It is an Early Gothic style area with yet another fine vault supported by clustered pillars. Other special features include:

St Swithun's Shrine The saint's remains were brought into the new cathedral in the 11th century. His shrine stood behind the high altar screen on a raised platform which still exists. There is no visual record of what the shrine might have looked like. The shrine was moved to the east end in the 15th century, but was destroyed in 1538 during the Reformation. The rudimentary modern shrine was installed in 1962, a thousand years after the saint's death. The design of the metal stand includes broken eggshells, which is a reference to the alleged miracle of St Swithun making broken eggs whole.

Holy Hole and icons

Holy Hole The series of handsome Russian icons from the 1990s are mounted at eye level on the east side of the wall of St Swithun's platform. Just below the Russian icons on this low west wall is an opening, the so-called 'Holy Hole.' In earlier times this aperture allowed pilgrims to crawl beneath St Swithun's platform and lie close to his tomb in hope of benefitting from his healing powers.

Free-standing Chantries Scattered around the east end are the large, carved stone chantries of three bishops and a cardinal. Each has a colored effigy of its occupant, and each chantry features an elaborately vaulted ceiling. All are fine examples of late Gothic design. They are:
- Bishop Fox's at the intersection of the south aisle and the east end.
- Bishop Gardiner's at the intersection of the north aisle and the east end. He was an opponent of the Reformation, was imprisoned, and then reinstated by Mary Tudor.
- Bishop Waynefleet's on the north side of the east end.
- Cardinal Beaufort's on the south side of the east end.

Joan of Arc Statue A lifelike statue of Joan of Arc was erected here in 1923 when she was canonized. The statue faces the Cardinal Beaufort chantry. The irony is that it was he who condemned her to death by burning at the stake in Rouen in 1431.

Enclosed Chapels Two fine chapels occupy each corner of the east end, adjacent to the Lady Chapel. Bishop Langton's altar tomb occupies the southeast corner. The carved wood frame and other woodwork on the tomb is handsome. However, the most interesting feature of this altar tomb is the ribbed and painted ceiling. Chapel of the Guardian Angels is at the northeast corner. This small chapel is notable for the 13th-century painted ceiling, with large- and medium-sized roundels depicting angels.

Bishop Langton tomb

WINCHESTER CATHEDRAL

Medieval Floor Tiles A rare feature here are these floor tiles. This area of the cathedral is covered with the most extensive set of medieval tiles in England.

➢ *Proceed to the Lady Chapel [Floor Plan #8].*

LADY CHAPEL

The Lady Chapel was completely remodeled into its present form around 1498. The highlights of this small chapel are the vaulted ceiling, decorated with bosses, and the large traceried east window. This 13th-century window was extensively remodeled in the 14th century, and again in about 1500.

Of equal interest are the beautiful early-16th-century wall paintings depicting miracles and legends associated with the Blessed Virgin Mary. Those now on display are reconstructions set behind protective panels.

➢ *Take the north choir aisle [Floor Plan #9], down the steps to the Chapel of the Holy Sepulcher on the left [Floor Plan #10].*

Holy Sepulcher mural

CHAPEL OF THE HOLY SEPULCHER

Nestled on the south side of the north transept is this small, cave-like chapel. Given its subdued light, one can just make out the 12th-century paintings, discovered only in 1960. These faint and partially damaged, but wonderful, paintings cover the walls and ceilings. They depict in faded yellowish tones Christ's descent from the cross and burial.

➢ *Enter the north transept [Floor Plan #11].*

NORTH TRANSEPT

The north transept is the earliest part of the cathedral and is in the Norman style. It is so different from most of the rest of the interior in

North transept

"Sound II" by Gormley

its pure, plain Norman-ness that we felt that we had walked into a different church. The flat wooden ceiling is painted and divided into squares, supported by large, dark beams. The notable windows here are by the Victorian Edward Burne-Jones, who created windows for many of England's Gothic cathedrals.

➢ *Walk down the steps to the crypt [Floor Plan #12].*

CRYPT

Also accessible via the north transept is the entrance to the often-flooded crypt. In it is a modern sculpture of a man, "Sound II," by Antony Gormley. He is standing, contemplating the water held in his cupped hands. The eerie quality of this lone figure in the empty crypt evokes a variety of feelings.

➢ *Exit via the west front.*

PROFILES OF THE 13 CHURCHES
EAST

King Henry VI, Canterbury

King's College Chapel, Cambridge

Three-quarter rear view

Personal Impressions

Cambridge is a bustling town, full of greenswards. But the real attractions are the many ancient colleges of Cambridge University and other old buildings with spires and towers over majestic doorways. The town is packed with tourists in season. While their numbers are substantial, the visitors don't overwhelm the experience in the town or inside the King's College Chapel.

Despite its reputation as "one of the finest examples of all Gothic architecture in the UK," we were not impressed by our first glimpse of the chapel from the outside. The tall, narrow rear façade viewed from the street looked ordinary. Much more interesting were the gatehouse entrance and the college compound.

The moment we walked into the chapel, however, we were awed. The first thing we saw was the spectacular, two-level, shiny dark-brown and gold organ atop the choir screen. Our attention was then drawn upwards to the 16th-century stained-glass windows which line the walls, and the towering fan-vaulted ceiling with its astounding stonework.

According to Britain Express, "King's College Chapel is arguably the most magnificent example of late medieval English architecture in the entire country. Guidebooks run out of superlatives to describe the richness of its interior decoration and structural elements." We could not agree more. The lovely singing amidst exquisitely carved choir stalls evoked spiritual feelings during evensong. This chapel is a marvel in every respect.

After exiting the chapel, a walk around the King's College compound was rewarding. This grassy compound extends from the large and handsome front gate on the main street to the Cam River. Walking it one passes by the wonderful old college buildings en route to the King's Bridge which spans the river, busy with flat boats (called "punts" in local parlance) full of visitors.

One unique building worth visiting in the town is a small 12th-century Norman church. Commemorating the Church of the Holy Sepulcher in Jerusalem, it is the oldest of the four extant round medieval churches in Britain.

History

Unlike any other English Gothic churches, King's Chapel is unique in that it was conceived, built, paid for, and tended to by five successive kings—not church or college officials—over a period of 100 years. While some kings played a greater role than others, all were significant. The first was Henry VI who reigned from 1422 to 1461. He was only 19 when he set the dimensions of the chapel in 1440, and laid the first stone, five years after the erection of King's College, Cambridge. He planned for Cambridge to have a close relationship with Eton College, which he also established in 1440. Given this history, King's College admitted for over 400 years only Etonians. At the time, Cambridge was still a port. To make space for his college, Henry obtained the needed land through "eminent domain," then tore down shops, lanes, and wharves, and even a church. It took three years to purchase and clear the land.

Then, in 1461, as an outcome of the Wars of the Roses, Henry VI was deposed by the new king, Edward IV, and was imprisoned in the Tower of London in 1465. All construction stopped, and Henry VI died in the tower in 1471. Edward IV gave the college some of the money that Henry VI had intended for his chapel. However, little construction was done in the years between Henry's imprisonment and the early death from illness of Edward IV in 1483. Richard III then became king but was killed by Henry VII in 1485 at the Battle of Bosworth Field. By the time of Richard III's death, five bays (sections of the nave set off by piers on each side) had been completed and a timber roof erected, despite the chaotic Wars of the Roses.

While visiting King's College in 1506 Henry VII left money to assure that the work could continue even after his death. He sent the money in the chest which can still be seen in the chapel.

In 1508 work resumed in earnest. By 1512 the shell of the chapel was finished and roofed in timber and lead. Henry VII's executors gave a further £5,000 to pay for the magnificent fan vaulting, and by 1515 the main structure was completed. The final work of creating and installing the great windows was not completed until 1531, and the early Renaissance choir was erected in 1532–1536. Henry VIII oversaw most of the glazing of the windows and funded the choir screen and much of the chapel's woodwork.

King's Chapel emerged unscathed during England's several religious upheavals. A serendipitous aspect of its history is that Henry VIII, who initiated the Reformation, was also the chapel's major sponsor.

The chapel also miraculously escaped serious damage during the Civil War, although one royalist observer claimed that in inclement weather the chapel was used as a parade ground by Cromwell's troops. Some suggest that Cromwell himself, a former Cambridge student, gave orders to spare the chapel.

It also escaped damage during World War II, when most of the glass was removed for safety. Only the west window remained in place.

Building

Exterior

The chapel has a unique shape for a medieval religious building: a long rectangle at 289 feet (88m) long by 40 feet (12m) wide. It has straight side walls

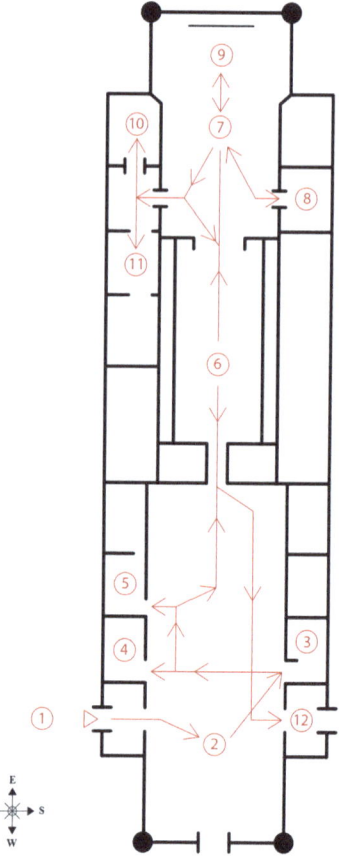

Floor Plan

1. Northwest portal
2. West end
3. Tomb chapel
4. Whichote chapel
5. Founder's chapel
6. Choir area
7. East end
8. Chapel of All Saints
9. Rubens painting
10. St Edward chapel
11. Exhibition chapel
12. Southwest portal

down to the ground level, where the side chapels project out from the upper walls. There are no transepts or other projections.

Exterior decoration is limited to the four low-rise octagonal towers, one at each corner. The edge of the roof is fitted with a line of decorated pinnacles. The north and south walls are a kaleidoscope of large clerestory windows which fill the walls with glass—12 per side—as well as the smaller windows in the side chapels at ground level. There are attached buttresses between each window opening. Both the west and east ends are dominated by enormous stained-glass windows, and the west front has many Tudor carvings above the single portal.

➢ *Enter the chapel via the north doorway near the front [Floor Plan #1].*

74   ENGLAND'S MARVELOUS GOTHIC CATHEDRALS AND CHURCHES

Interior

King's College Chapel has only a single aisle down the middle, and there are neither piers nor arcades. The chapel has a two-level elevation: the dominant upper clerestory level is filled with massive, beautiful windows, while the lower level is lined with a series of side chapels. Oddly for a medieval religious building in England, the chapel has few memorials.

There is a stark division—physically and symbolically—between the west and east ends of the chapel interior. For example, under the instructions of the austere and pious Henry VI, the east end (from the choir to the east wall) is almost totally lacking in any carving or other decorations. One might call this the "religious" arm. By contrast, the west end, completed by Henry VIII, lacks any religious symbols. Instead it is highly decorated by a proliferation of stone and wood carvings, all or nearly all celebrating the Tudor dynasty. This could be called the "secular" arm.

Two features dominate the interior: the ceiling and the windows. Take the time to read about them before commencing the walk-through.

CEILING

The inspirational, intricate fan-vaulted ceiling is the world's largest, and soars upwards before exploding into a series of stone fireworks. The fan vault is decorated with carved bosses of wood and stone, with images of heraldic beasts, coats of arms, and Tudor motifs. As the story goes, the original vault was to be of the earlier less-complex ribbed variety. It is our good luck that the master mason appointed in 1512 opted for the superb fan vaulting that one sees today. Some side chapels also feature fan vaulting.

WINDOWS

The windows in the chapel comprise the finest and most complete collection of early-16th-century glass in England. They were made using a mix of the stained and hand-painted techniques. The contrast between these windows and the earlier medieval ones in other English Gothic churches is obvious. The windows here are "painterly," full of movement, and committed to a complex narrative from panel to panel.

There are 26 main windows in the chapel: 12 large clerestory windows on each of the north and south walls; and the even larger east and west windows. Most were made by Flemish and English artisans from 1515 to 1531.

Clerestory Windows Each of these 24 windows — at 36 feet (11m) tall — is divided horizontally by a stone mullion, with five glass panels in each level. The upper panels represent scenes from the Old Testament, which foreshadow the events in the lower panels. Both vertical center glass panels depict prophets, saints, and angels.

A nicely illustrated booklet — available at the shop — walks visitors through the stories narrated in all these upper windows.

These windows are not easy to "read," especially for those without a good knowledge of the Old and New Testaments, and a pair of binoculars. The story-telling starts with the window over the entrance on the north side (Window 1: Mary's birth as part of God's plan), then continues down the north wall, around the east end, and back west to the window 25 (Mary's Assumption and her coronation as Queen of Heaven) over the exit on the south side.

East Window This large window has 18 tall glass panels, nine in the lower half and nine in the upper half. Overall this window features six scenes from the New Testament depicting the death of Jesus. The top nine panels tell the story of the Crucifixion, while the bottom nine depict how Pontius Pilate dealt with the accusations against Jesus by the Jewish religious leaders. This window was installed in 1540 near the end of Henry VIII's reign.

West window

West Window Sitting above the west front main door, the west window had only plain glass at the time of Henry VIII's death in 1547. The present window was donated and installed in the late 19th century. It depicts the Last Judgment: The upper part shows Christ in glory surrounded by angels, apostles, and saints. St Michael armed with the scales of justice is shown in the lower part. Those headed for Heaven are on the left, while those headed for Hell are on the right.

➢ *Begin the walk through the interior, from front to back [Floor Plan #2].*

WEST END

The highlights in this part of the chapel include the carved Tudor emblems and side chapels. The Tudor emblems represent the following:
- Fleur-de-Lys: a symbol of the English king's claim to the throne of France
- Tudor Rose (the combined red and white roses of Lancaster and York): a symbol of the Tudor union of these dynasties
- Dragon: Henry VII's reminder that his Tudor father was Welsh
- Tudor coats of arms
- Greyhound: a symbol of loyalty, and also the emblem of Henry VII's mother's family
- Portcullis: Henry VII's royal blood through his mother.

Only a few side chapels are open and three are worthy of attention.

Tomb Chapel [Floor Plan #3] This chapel is notable for its collection of memorials and fan-vaulted ceiling. Of special interest is the window depicting Henry VI as king and religious leader.

Whichote Chapel [Floor Plan #4] It has a wonderful ribbed ceiling and a fine altar painting of the Virgin and Child. It is used for baptism of members of the college.

Founder's Chapel [Floor Plan #5] It is notable for another fine vaulted ceiling, a painted triptych on the altar, and a larger painting near the door.

➢ *Proceed to the choir area [Floor Plan #6].*

CHOIR AREA

Choir Screen A superbly carved dark oak screen dominates the center of the chapel. It was erected 1532–1536 by Henry VIII in celebration of his marriage to Anne Boleyn. Look for the king's initials "HR" (Henricus Rex) entwined with those of Anne Boleyn "RA" (Regina Anna). Ironically, he had her executed at about the same time as the screen was finished. The screen is an example of early Renaissance design and is a striking contrast to the Perpendicular design in the rest of the chapel. It is said to be the most exquisite piece of Italian decoration in England.

Organ The very large "bat wing" organ perched dramatically on top of the choir screen contrasts the dark oak case with gleaming brass pipes. The organ case was built from 1686–1688. The two stunning angels which grace the top of the organ were the last of several decorations in that location, installed only in 1859. As with most organs in old churches, this one has been rebuilt and refurbished a number of times over the years.

Choir Stalls The Tudor choir stalls were made by the same carver who did the screen. The canopies behind the stalls contain the finely carved 1633 heraldic panels which show the arms of different kings and queens, as well as depictions of biblical stories. For example, note the central panel, depicting St George killing the dragon. The canopies were carved later, between 1675 and 1678.

Choir screen and organ

➢ *Proceed into the east end [Floor Plan #7].*

EAST END

Compared with the chapels in the west end, the three side chapels at this end are simple with plain stone-vaulted ceilings. The Flemish or Rhenish windows inside these chapels date from about 1530 but were installed here in the 20th century.

➢ *Start at the Chapel of All Souls on the right [Floor Plan # 8].*

Chapel of All Souls (aka The Memorial Chapel) This chapel serves as a memorial for the members of the college and choir killed in the two world wars. The ceiling and several stained-glass windows with fine tracery are noteworthy. The window depicts Mary bottle-feeding a Unicorn. Note also the coats of arms of Sts Catherine and Margaret mounted on the doorway arch leading to this chapel.

Magi painting by Rubens St Edward Chapel

➤ *Continue to the Rubens painting in the center [Floor Plan # 9].*

Rubens Painting Behind the high altar and directly under the east window is Peter Paul Rubens painting, "Adoration of the Magi." Originally painted for a Belgian convent, it was acquired by a British nobleman, then passed through several families before being donated to King's. It was installed in the chapel in 1968. This valuable painting was vandalized in 1974 with the letters IRA scratched across it. Fortunately, the damage was repairable, albeit at a high cost.

Chapels on the North Wall The two chapels here are accessed through a single doorway, whose arch is decorated with three handsome coats of arms: St Edmund, Edward the Confessor, and the Royal Arms.

St Edward Chapel [Floor Plan #10]. This chapel may be set aside for private prayer. Above the altar is a luminous painting of the Madonna and Child.

Exhibition Chapel [Floor Plan #11]. This long and narrow chapel features an exhibition on the history of King's Chapel. It is spread out among several contiguous rooms.

➤ *Exit via the southwest portal [Floor Plan #12].*

Ely Cathedral

West front

Personal Impressions

Ely is a small town in the heart of the Fens, the low marshy areas of Cambridgeshire. The name Ely is thought to come from an old word meaning "district of eels," and eels are still supposed to be a delicacy of the area.

Ely Cathedral is situated in a rather quiet neighborhood. Since the cathedral is surrounded by a greensward with no compound wall or tall buildings, the view is unimpeded. From the outside, the chopped-off left side and the odd towers on the right side slightly diminish the dramatic effect of the west front. This tall and vertical west front with its large multi-stepped central tower is an exercise in unrestrained exuberance. Every surface is packed with intersecting arched windows and openings.

The highlight of the interior is the painted wood ceiling of the unique 14th-century octagonal lantern tower. There are also the beautiful choir with its many humorous carvings on the old stalls and the flamboyant screen behind the high altar. The unrestricted view from the west end all the way to the east is remarkable.

After climbing the many stairs to the landing surrounding the lantern tower ceiling, we peered down through the painted doors. What we saw of the interior from here is awe-inspiring. Charged with excitement, we continued our climb up the 175 very narrow stone steps to the roof. What a view of the countryside! The quiet small town and this marvelous cathedral make for a memorable visit to Ely.

History

The present cathedral replaced the original 675 CE monastery founded by St Etheldreda. Originally built in the Norman style, the galilee porch, Lady Chapel, and choir were then rebuilt in the exuberant Decorated style. Ely has few examples of the later Perpendicular style, except in some of the smaller chapels, and one or two windows. Over the years, weak foundations resulted in the collapse of the northwest transept and central tower. A variety of bracing and other expedients have been employed to stabilize the building.

During Henry VIII's Reformation, the shrines to the Anglo-Saxon saints were destroyed, along with essentially all the stained glass and all the free-standing statues. In the Lady Chapel all 147 carved figures in the frieze of the Virgin Mary were decapitated, as were many sculptures in the Bishop West chapel. In the mid-19th century, almost all the windows in the cathedral—over 100—were re-glazed with colored glass, since none of the medieval glass remained, except for a few fragments in the Lady Chapel. After the Reformation, the passageway into the Lady Chapel was turned into a poorhouse. The entire east end was used as a place for burials and memorials, and the cathedral was downgraded to a mere parish church until 1938.

For many churches, the Civil War period was as bad as the Reformation. Throughout the 1640s, Cromwell's army occupied Ely. The bishop spent 18 years in the Tower of London.

Perhaps because the damage had been so extensive during the Reformation, there was relatively little damage done to the cathedral during the Civil War, except for the demolition of the cloister and chapter house.

Although the Parliament had decided to demolish the entire Ely complex, it is rumored that Oliver Cromwell himself stepped in to protect it. Cromwell locked the cathedral for 17 years—a blessing which may have protected it from serious damage. It may be no coincidence that Cromwell's family home is located close to the cathedral.

A series of restorations were carried out towards the end of the 17th century. These included mounting a fine organ case with trumpeting angels on the Norman stone choir screen. Soon after, a corner of the north transept collapsed and had to be rebuilt. The rebuild faithfully reinstated the Norman walls, windows, and detailing. This was a landmark approach in the history of restoration.

In the late-18th century, a combination of clergy and lay architects carried out a series of largely essential repairs and also made "improvements." These included repairing the decayed octagonal lantern tower. By moving the choir stalls east of the crossing, the octagon-crossing became a spacious and dramatic public area, with grand vistas to east and west, and a spectacular view of the octagon vaulting. The restorers also removed the Norman choir screen and put in a new screen east of the crossing, onto which they mounted the 17th-century organ case. Despite these improvements, they dismantled at least some of the choir stalls, and did away with the old choir screen, with little regard for their historic value.

George Scott was brought in to re-work the 14th-century choir stalls. He moved them back towards the crossing but kept the crossing open space. He also installed a new carved wooden choir screen with brass gates and moved the high altar westwards. In addition, he installed a lavishly carved and ornamented alabaster high altar screen. His other renovations included: a new font in the southwest transept; a new organ case; and a new nave pulpit, replacing the neo-Norman pulpit. Still other restorers installed the present wooden ceiling in the nave, painted with scenes from the Old and New Testaments. They also repainted the interior of the lantern tower ceiling. Today it is impossible to judge which of these many changes were beneficial and which were not.

Building

At 537 feet (164m) long, Ely is the fourth longest English cathedral. This provokes the question why such a large church was built in such a small village. One must assume that size decisions were based more on the power and wealth of the local monastic community, or merchants, than on population size.

The plan of the building is cruciform thanks to the transept at the crossing, which projects far from the cathedral walls. Only the southwest transept at the west front is extant. As noted, the cloister and chapter house at Ely were destroyed during the Civil War.

Although there are many shrines at Ely, the only interesting ones, architecturally speaking, are those of several early bishops and two saints. Ely is distinctive in having fewer chapels, monuments, and shrines than most, although the area east of the choir has some tombs and memorials.

Exterior

FRONT

The west front was a departure from its Norman design. It is richly decorated with intersecting arches and complex moldings. Note the rows of quatrefoil openings and use of pointed instead of semicircular arches. This multi-level west front displays a high level of order and uniformity. However, the additional side building with its crenellated round towers creates a lopsided look which distracts from the elegance of the main west front.

The 13th-century Early Gothic galilee porch projects out from the west front. The term galilee means a porch or entrance, the name originating from the place where Jesus left for Jerusalem. The doorway is graceful, its main arch divided into two sub-arches separated by a slender pillar. Although the original liturgical functions of this porch are not known, its location at the west entrance suggests that it was used as a chapel for penitents; a place where liturgical processions could gather; or where the monks could hold consultations with women, who were not permitted inside. The tall lancet windows are set above the galilee porch.

TOWERS

There are only two towers: the single west tower and the central lantern tower.

West Tower The west tower, erected in 1400, adds to the exuberance of the west front. With a height of 215 feet (66m), this single tower is one of the

Central tower

tallest among English cathedrals. Numerous attempts were made to correct instability problems due to the subsidence of the soft ground.

Central Lantern Tower The original central tower collapsed into the choir in 1322 and was replaced with this octagonal tower with a height of 141 feet (43m). At 71 feet (22m) wide, the tower opening was too wide to support a stone vaulted ceiling below. Thus, this vaulted ceiling had to be constructed of wood. This massive tower has two levels, the topmost of which juts up like a crown. This amazing octagonal structure is undoubtedly unique to Ely Cathedral.

Interior

➢ *Enter through the west front [Floor Plan #1] and into the west tower gallery [Floor Plan #2].*

WEST TOWER GALLERY

After passing through the entrance, visitors should look up to see the square painting of Jesus, surrounded by angels, holding an orb—the world—in his hands. There are three arcaded windows on each of the four sides of the west tower.

➢ *Enter the nave [Floor Plan #3].*

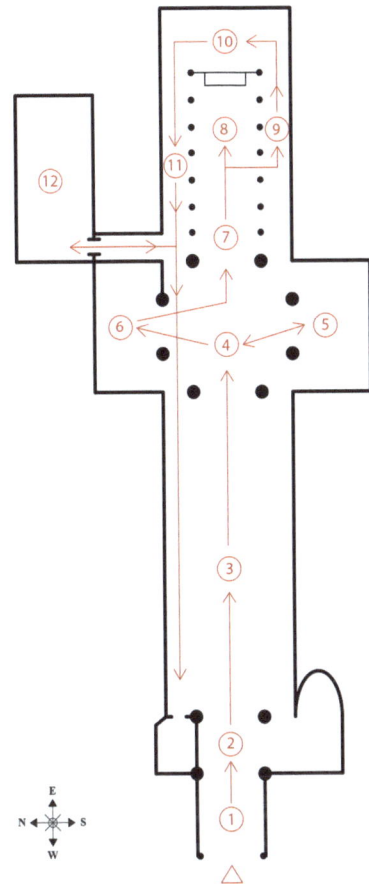

Floor Plan

1. West front
2. West tower gallery
3. Nave
4. Crossing
5. South transept
6. North transept
7. Choir area
8. High altar area
9. South choir aisle
10. East end
11. North choir aisle
12. Lady Chapel

NAVE

Standing just inside, one can see all the way down the nave to the east window, a wonderful sight. The nave is only 70 feet (22m) high, one of the lowest among English Gothic churches. By contrast, at a length of 246 feet (75m), this nave may be one of the longest in any early English church. Elevation levels consist of the standard arcade, triforium, and clerestory. The triforium has a central pillar with rounded arches, while the glazed clerestory is similar, although with two pillars. Nave piers are a hybrid of the simple, round Norman design, but with the Early Gothic addition of attached shafts. A single shaft rises from the floor alongside each pier to join the ceiling. The nave arches are plain and rounded, with deeply cut molding.

ELY CATHEDRAL

West Windows There are, in effect, two sets of west windows: On the exterior, there are the three tall lancet windows set above the galilee porch. And then, inside the nave entry is the beautiful eight-panel stained-glass window with tracery at the top. It sits on the west nave wall, immediately above the doorway leading from the galilee porch to the interior. Like nearly all windows at Ely, these windows are Victorian replacements.

West Transept The nave originally had northwest and southwest transepts. The northwest transept collapsed in the 15th century due to weak foundations. A great sloping pile of masonry was built to buttress the existing walls, which remain outside on the north side of the tower. This former transept space is now used for the cathedral shop and café. The remaining southwest transept may be one of England's most ornate Norman interiors with its fine series of blind arches and marvelous painted ceiling. The mid-19th-century font is also located here.

A stairway from this space leads to the Stained Glass Museum, which offers insights into the 800-year history and techniques of British stained glass. A touch-screen virtual museum visit is available through an interactive display on the ground floor.

Ceiling A simply amazing painted, concave, wooden ceiling runs the full length of the nave. It was installed in the mid-19th century and painted by two artists with scenes from the Old and New Testaments in stunning light pastel greens and pinkish reds. The interior of the octagon was also repainted during this period.

Prior's Door and Monks' Door The south wall of the nave is distinctive for its two 1135 Norman doors: the Prior's Door and the Monk's Door. The more interesting of these is the former, decorated with tendrils, figures, and other motifs. It is arched with a trefoil design and multiple Norman carvings. The tympanum over the door depicts Christ attended by angels with large hands and feet. Most of the decoration of this door is on the outside in a room off the nave aisle.

Southwest transept ceiling

Octagon ceiling

Nave looking east

View from octagon gallery

➢ *Continue into the crossing [Floor Plan #4].*

OCTAGONAL CROSSING AND TOWER

The east end of the nave opens into the great octagonal crossing with its dramatic painted ceiling—the most important feature of the cathedral. The ceiling design is an eight-pointed star with flaring ribs. At the center is a representation of Christ on a wooden boss carved from a single piece of oak. The boss is surrounded by 32 wooden panels of painted angels playing instruments. These panels can be opened so choristers can sing from here. Tours of the tower allow visitors to look down from these panels to see the splendid view below, especially the intricate tile floors.

While the upper octagon tower is stone, the lantern tower is lead-covered wood. Above the ceiling is a secondary supporting structure, consisting of rare but hidden hammer-beam supports. This is England's earliest use of hammer-beam construction. Even more interesting are the vertical supports consisting of eight huge, hidden, medieval oak beams, 63 feet (19m) long and three to four feet thick (0.91 to 1.22m). The enormous open area is 142 feet (43m) high and 69 feet (21m) wide. This massive vertical construction is supported by eight gigantic piers with triangular windows at each of the four corner junctions. Note the handsome carved stone pulpit to the left near the choir screen.

➤ *Proceed into the south transept [Floor Plan #5].*

MAIN TRANSEPT

The main transept arm flanks the enormous octagonal crossing to the north and south. Built at the beginning of the 12th century, these transepts are the oldest parts of the cathedral. The matching original ceilings were replaced in the mid-15th century with painted hammer-beam ceilings, decorated with flying angels. Hammer-beam ceilings are rare in medieval cathedrals, and these are very beautiful.

South Transept Things of interest here include the chapel dedicated to two 10th-century sainted bishops, Dunstan and Ethelwold, who began the monastery here which lasted until it was dissolved by Henry VIII.

There is a modern sculpture on the south wall and two, easy-to-miss, paintings. The painting at the top depicts an atmospheric Angel and St Peter. Of greater interest is the painting just under it, the so-called 'Eliensis Painting,' all dark colors and small figures. These figures are a mix of Norman knights and monks after a battle.

➤ *Cross over to the north transept [Floor Plan #6].*

Hammer-beam ceiling, south transept

North Transept This transept has two interesting chapels. First is the 14th-century St Edmund's chapel, notable for its well-preserved medieval murals depicting the martyrdom of St Edmund by the Vikings. The second, St George's chapel, commemorates the Cambridgeshire Regiment.

➢ *Enter the choir area [Floor Plan #7].*

CHOIR AREA

Choir Screen The screen separates the octagonal crossing from the choir. The modern oak choir screen was installed by the ubiquitous George Scott. It replaced the massive Norman screen destroyed in 1760.

Choir Stalls The rear rows of the choir stalls are 14th century, with finely carved misericords. Since the stalls were defaced in the Reformation, much of what remains is Victorian. The canopies above the stalls have a series of 19th-century carvings with scenes from the Old and New Testaments.

Organ A new organ case was installed on the choir wall by George Scott. Decorated with trumpeting angels and other embellishments, it is modeled after the medieval organ at Strasbourg Cathedral. Curiously, the organ case has no working pipes inside—they are installed inside the adjacent triforium.

Ceiling The choir ceiling's fine, complex design has multiple dark-colored intersecting ribs, which contrast with the lighter background. Bosses abound.

➢ *Continue to the high altar area [Floor Plan #8].*

HIGH ALTAR AREA

Altar Screen The piers, arches, and upper windows in this area are an exercise in Gothic decorative exuberance. The "Italian style" marble altar screen was designed by George Scott. Its five panels depict the events during the last week of Jesus' life from his entry into Jerusalem on Palm Sunday to his death on Good Friday. The central panel shows the Last Supper.

Ceiling These dramatic ceiling ribs spring from the wall-mounted shafts on both walls. Bundles of ribs flare out into a triangular

Last Supper detail, altar screen

ELY CATHEDRAL

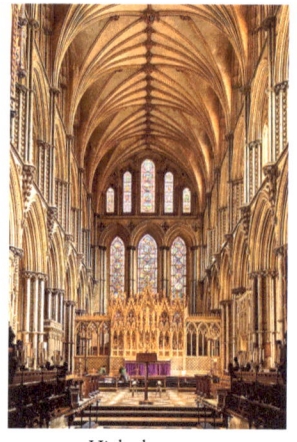

High altar area

shape to meet at the continuous ridge rib at the apex, which runs east and west.

Memorials Two memorials in the high altar area are of interest: one sad, one infuriating. The sad memorial is the simple black stone set in the floor, marking the original location of St Etheldreda's pilgrim shrine. The infuriating memorial is the brass plaque in the floor of the south choir aisle commemorating Bishop Goodrich. During the Reformation, the bishop destroyed all the medieval statues, paintings, and stained glass in the cathedral. Nothing remains of Ely's medieval decoration, including Etheldreda's shrine, which he also destroyed. His memorial plaque is now roped off; perhaps in case a hostile visitor from the past should show up. Fortunately, St Etheldreda has a dedicated chapel in the east end.

➢ *Exit to the south choir aisle [Floor Plan #9], and enter the east end [Floor Plan #10].*

EAST END

The many pilgrims in the 13th century drawn to St Etheldreda's shrine led to the addition of the east end, done in Early Gothic design.

Bishop West Chapel This chapel is at the southeast corner. Of special note are its elaborate Renaissance ceiling and heavily carved walls.

St Etheldreda's Chapel and East Windows The central space at the east end is dedicated to St Etheldreda, Ely Cathedral's founder. The east windows in the chapel consist of three tall lancets in the middle and five smaller upper ones. The tall windows tell the story of Jesus: his birth, his ministry, and the last week of his life. The five smaller ones depict the Resurrection with Christ ascending in glory. Like virtually all glass at Ely, they are Victorian.

Bishop Alcock Chapel At the northeast corner, the 13th-century Bishop John Alcock chapel has a stunning fan-vaulted ceiling with rare pendants and intricate wall carvings.

➢ *Take the north choir aisle [Floor Plan #11], and turn right into the passageway to the Lady Chapel [Floor Plan #12].*

Bishop Alcock chapel

LADY CHAPEL

This semi-detached Lady Chapel in the Decorated style is reputed to be the largest—100 feet (30m) long—and to have the widest at 46 feet (14m) medieval vault in England. Begun in 1321, the original chapel was highly colored, with painted statues in the niches, and fitted with brightly colored stained glass throughout. All the old windows were lost over time, replaced by the current Victorian glass.

The north and south walls are punctuated by five bays, separated by slender piers, and retain the niches and canopies which once held statues. The ceiling has a remarkably handsome and complex rib design and has many bosses.

The stone seats which line the walls are topped with elaborately carved canopies, decorated with figures and foliage. At the upper triangular intersection of each arch (spandrel) are scenes with 93 carved relief sculptures of the Virgin Mary. Since the chapel highlights the Virgin, the Protestants destroyed most of the carvings.

Frieze

➢ *Exit via the west front.*

ELY CATHEDRAL

Peterborough Cathedral

Personal Impressions

This marvelous cathedral is hard to see from afar, or even when close. We almost got lost walking to it. The small cathedral compound is surrounded by a huge shopping mall and shops in the center of this rather plain town. We finally found the ancient gate into the compound with its spacious and pleasant front lawn. We later learned that had we come from a different direction, we could have entered via the main, front entrance.

Facing the cathedral, the first thing we noticed was its unusual west front. It looks as if someone had scooped out three deep, vertical recesses in the front and put a small, odd-looking gilded box at ground level in the center. It is surely different from any "normal" church fronts. Strangely, once we got used to it, we warmed to its uniqueness.

West front

The interior has many special treats, including the Norman-dominated design of nearly every architectural feature and the lovely high altar screen. As history fans, we loved the tombs of the two famous queens: Catherine of Aragon and Mary Queen of Scots. But most of all, it's the ceilings: everywhere one turns there is another incredible ceiling, each one different and special.

After experiencing the eye-opening ceilings throughout the cathedral, It was worth spending time outside the cathedral to see the site of the former cloister with the oldest stone wall, the monks' dormitory, and the chapter house. The original structures are all gone, but the serene remnants still speak to us of the history of this fine national monument. Just sitting in the remnants of the old cloister on a sunny morning gave us all the calm we needed for the hectic schedule we had.

History

The original church was founded in about 655 CE, making it one of the first centers of Christianity in this region. The area, including the church, was attacked by the Vikings in 864 CE and again in 870 CE. They razed the church and slaughtered the monks. In the mid-10th century, the Benedictines built an abbey on this site. Damaged during the Norman invasion, the abbey was repaired but was destroyed by a fire in 1116. This resulted in the current building in the Norman style in 1118, and it was consecrated in 1238. The abbey was dissolved during the Reformation in 1539, and two years later became a cathedral with a new bishop.

The Lady Chapel was built at the end of the 13th century, at which time the Norman windows were replaced with Decorated ones. During the 14th century, more changes were made: the central lantern tower was erected with a wooden octagonal top; the triforium windows were transformed into the Decorated style; and the small porch was added to the west front. Several Norman windows were fitted with Perpendicular tracery later in the 15th century. Except for the late-15th-century addition to the east end, the structure of the building remains basically the same as it was when consecrated.

Existing mid-12th-century records list the abbey's relics as having included a mind-boggling (and skeptic-inducing) collection of exotic religious items, such as the swaddling clothes of baby Jesus; pieces of Jesus' manger; fragments of the five loaves which fed Jesus' followers; a piece of clothing of the Virgin

Mary; and relics of Sts Paul and Andrew. The relics were assumed to be lost following the Dissolution. Just before the Reformation this cathedral had the sixth largest monastic income in England and had a large number of monks.

Henry VIII's first wife, Catherine of Aragon, was buried here in 1536. Perhaps due to his guilt over his treatment of her, he spared the abbey from most Reformation damage.

However, the cathedral was vandalized by Cromwell's men during the Civil War. Almost all the stained glass, the medieval choir stalls, the high altar and its screen, the Lady Chapel, and the chapter house were demolished. Only the south and west walls of the cloister court remain. The 13th-century monks' infirmary, which consisted of a hall with aisles and an altar, was demolished. The aisles were used as cells or couches for the sick monks. On the south are the remains of the monastery. The monks' dormitory, kitchen, and refectory components of the monastery's remains are situated further south beyond the cloister walls.

Some of the damage was repaired during the 17th and 18th centuries. Extensive renovations were done in the late-19th century, which included rebuilding the piers, the choir, and the west front. In addition, new hand-carved choir stalls, the bishop's throne, and choir-area pulpit were installed. The marble pavement and high altar were also added.

In 2001 an arsonist set the nave on fire. The timing was particularly unfortunate as a complete restoration of the painted wooden ceiling was nearing completion. The oily smoke coated much of the building with a sticky black layer.

Building

This cathedral, together with Durham and Ely cathedrals, is one of the few intact 12th-century buildings in England, despite changes over the centuries. It is notable for the far greater length of the west end versus the east end. The nave from the west portal to the east side of the crossing has nine bays, versus only five in the east end. Other interesting architectural features are the distinctive rounded apse end, which surrounds the high altar area, a holdover from the cathedral's Norman origin. In addition, the choir area sits entirely in the nave, west of the crossing.

The cathedral has two sets of transepts: The main set is at the crossing, while the smaller, insignificant set is just inside the west front. They are almost entirely of Norman design: the piers and arches are decorated with a variety of carvings.

Exterior

WEST FRONT

During the 13th-century rebuild, the abbot erected a new west front in the Gothic style on top of the existing Norman front. It is said that he did this after seeing the new Gothic choir at Canterbury. The entire Early Gothic front we now see was pretty much just tacked on, like a Hollywood movie set. Evidence for this is compelling. To hold the new west front in place, a steel cable was inserted from front to back, and tied on each side to these brackets. Take a minute to spot the small, white-metal façade-support brackets: one at the intersection (spandrel) of each of the three arched recesses, plus the series of small round ones just below the decorative horizontal band (aka string course) across the upper level. The curious visitor can spot the corresponding interior brackets on the inner wall of the west front.

The present façade is unlike any other with its three tall arched, very deep, recesses. Behind the Gothic front on the left (north) side is the northwest tower left over from the earlier front. The appearance of the west end is asymmetrical, as the south tower was never completed above a stubby base, but this is only visible from a distance. A carved string course runs along the top of the three main recessed arches, and below it the spandrels are decorated with trefoils, quatrefoils, and niches with statues. Above the carved stone line are a series of arches, some of which have statues. Each of the three gables across the top has a circular window of beautiful design, and there is a cross at the apex of each gable.

Standing in front, one's eye is immediately drawn to the small 14th-century "porch" structure inserted at the bottom of the central arch. This arched entry may have had three functions: to give additional strength to the west front; to act as a kind of buttress for the piers of the central arch; and perhaps to serve as a kind of gathering place for priests prior to processions. On top of this porch is a room which is now used as a library. The six-panel window in the library has a bowed "X-shaped" tracery across the upper level. The ceiling just inside the porch is a stone vault with a boss that represents the Trinity.

Deep inside the somewhat narrow central arched recess is the large but hard-to-see, heavily traceried, west front window. Both recessed arches are fitted with lancet windows.

Facing the cathedral, note the gateway to the left of the west front. This gateway, which leads to the Dean's residence, is highly ornamented with emblems such as the Tudor rose and portcullis.

TOWERS

The cathedral has only two towers: the full-sized northwest tower and the low-rise central lantern tower. The southwest tower was never finished and does not rise to the level of the roof line.

In addition, there are two square mini towers, one on each side of the façade. They rise in six windowless stages. Note the difference in their decoration: the one on the left has a plain spire, with pinnacles rising on each corner, while the one on the right has a faceted spire and pinnacles rising from arches.

Northwest Tower This 143-feet (44m) tall, square tower rises immediately behind the north gable on the west front. It has a row of lancet windows at the upper, belfry level and three pillared arches below. It also has a tall pinnacle at each of its four corners. Due to weak foundations resulting from the draining of the surrounding marshes, the entire west end of the cathedral was thought to be in danger of falling. This may be why only this 14th-century tower was completed. By default, the northwest tower is the location of the cathedral's bells. This tower was rebuilt in 1884 due to ongoing foundation concerns.

Central Lantern Tower The original central tower is reported to have been far larger than the present tower. As with the western towers, there was a concern about its stability, and it was reduced in height and weight in the mid-14th century. Above the lantern had been a wooden octagon. From the outside, the great length of the nave is emphasized by the position of the central tower at the end of the nave. Each face of the tower has two large lancet windows. It is surmounted by a crenellated parapet.

NEW BUILDING

Architecturally, the east end is rather peculiar. The original rounded Norman apse is still there, with its traceried windows. Below and behind it is this "new" eastern construction, added in the early-16th century in the late Perpendicular style. The addition simply extended the eastern walls and squared off the east end. It is richly ornamented. Twelve buttresses, attached to the walls between the windows, support these exterior walls. At the top of each is a seated statue of an apostle.

INTERIOR

➢ *Via the west front [Floor Plan #1], enter the nave [Floor Plan #2].*

East end

NAVE

In the English tradition, the nave typically emphasizes length over height. Its measurements here are 481 feet (147m) long, 206 feet (63m) wide, and with a nave height of 81 feet (25m). These dimensions place Peterborough in the mid-range of English medieval churches. The nave has 10 bays with Norman arches, a double-arched triforium, and a traceried clerestory with three stepped arches. The arcade arches are beautifully decorated with Norman carvings,

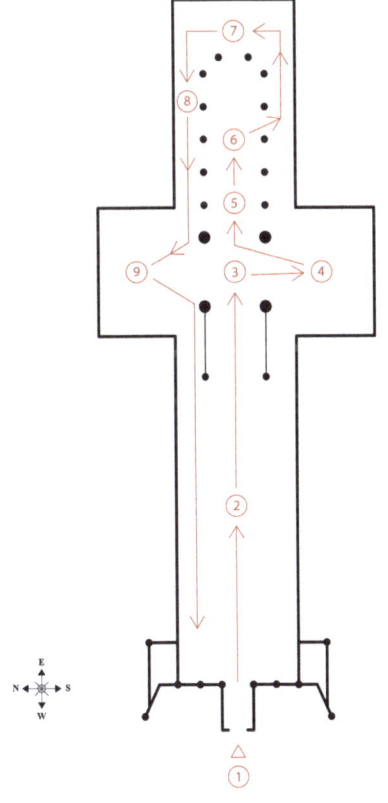

Floor Plan

1. West front
2. Nave
3. Crossing
4. Main south transept
5. Choir area
6. High altar area
7. New building
8. North choir aisle
9. Main north transept

and every level has glazed windows. The undecorated piers have alternating round and octagonal designs and have plain square-cut capitals. A single shaft ascends from the pier capitals to intersect with the ceiling.

Ceiling The main focus in the nave is the painted wooden Norman ceiling which covers the entire nave. The design depicts various figures such as kings, saints, animals, monsters, and musical instruments within lozenge-shaped medallions. It was created in the mid-13th century and has been repainted twice: once in 1745, then again in 1834.

Nave ceiling detail

Magically, it still retains the character and style of the original. The aisle ceilings were vaulted by Norman builders.

Gravedigger On the inner wall of the west front stands an old painting of the cathedral's resident 16th-century gravedigger, named Robert Scarlett, aka Old Scarlett. Legend has it that he buried both of the queens interred here and that he may have been the model for Shakespeare's gravedigger in *Hamlet*.

West Window This window sits above the roof of the low porch, deep in the recess formed by the central arch. Hard to see from outside, this large stained-glass window has five vertical panels divided about mid-level. The top is all beautiful late Gothic tracery. The present window was installed at the end of the 19th century and is dedicated to soldiers from the area who died in the Boer War. The figures depicted include kings, saints, and bishops.

Font Note the 13th-century font which stands near the entrance. The font basin is made of local marble, while the lower part is modern. Although not dramatic, this font is a handsome addition to the nave.

➢ *Continue to the crossing [Floor Plan #3].*

CROSSING

On the nave side of the crossing hangs a large and dramatic, bright red, crucifix, with Jesus on the Cross, erected in 1975. Above the crossing is the elevated ceiling of the square lantern tower. The walls of the lantern have two traceried windows on each side. The ceiling uses an elaborate rib design fanning out

Ceilings: transept, lantern tower, high altar, and choir

from each side of the square, forming an octagon shape in the center. The entire construction is beautifully painted and is embellished with gilt bosses.

➢ *Proceed to the main south transept [Floor Plan #4].*

MAIN TRANSEPTS

The main north and south transepts share many similarities. Notably, they both have some of the finest Norman architecture in England; abundant Perpendicular tracery; and three tiers of semicircular-headed windows with a wall-arcade below the lowest tier. Some 19th-century windows are by artists associated with the William Morris Arts and Crafts Movement. In addition, these transepts are fitted with beautiful, unpainted wood-paneled ceilings, which are original.

This south transept houses three small chapels, set off by medieval wooden screens. The only one of interest is St Oswald chapel, which has an unusual watchtower where a monk stood watch over the relic of St Oswald's arm. His arm disappeared from here at the time of the Reformation, despite the guard.

➢ *Enter the choir area [Floor Plan #5].*

CHOIR AREA

Choir Screen The original choir screen was destroyed in the 18th century and was not replaced. At that time, the choir was moved west of the crossing and into the nave.

Ceiling Since the choir area is set in the nave, the painted wood ceiling is over the choir area as well.

Choir Stalls and Other Fittings Nearly all fittings in the choir, including the choir stalls, are 19th century. It is believed that Peterborough originally had over 30 misericords from the 14th century; only three now survive. The walls behind the choir stalls are decorated with raised shields and are topped with heavily carved canopies. Some stalls have the coats of arms of a donor, or some other symbol, such as the six-pointed star emblem. Note the eagle lectern, which dates from the late-15th century. The choir area is also fitted with some exquisite carved wooden panels.

Organ This organ case and pipes are mounted on the north wall above the stalls. The instrument is purely ornamental with non-functioning pipes. The "real" pipes are in the triforium above. Due to damage from the 2001 fire, the organ was given a full-scale rebuild.

➢ *Proceed to the high altar area [Floor Plan #6].*

High altar baldachin

HIGH ALTAR AREA

The high altar area is inside the rounded apse. The area has several interesting features.

Bishop's Throne The tall Bishop's Throne is on the south wall, east of the choir area. It is constructed of dark wood, heavily carved with a Gothic design, all pinnacles and spires.

Pulpit Carved in dark wood and on two levels, the pulpit sits across the aisle from the Bishop's Throne. In the niches at the base are depictions of four abbots. Around the main body of the pulpit are those of Sts Peter, Paul, John, and James. Between these niches are wide panels carved with subjects associated with preaching.

High Altar Baldachin The altar is enclosed in an elaborate neo-Gothic baldachin (a ceremonial canopy of stone, metal, or fabric over an altar, throne, or doorway) made from pink marble. Although a magnificent piece of work, the flamboyant design seems a bit out of place. The three levels of stained-glass windows in the upper apse wall and in the new building addition in the east end can be seen through and above the baldachin.

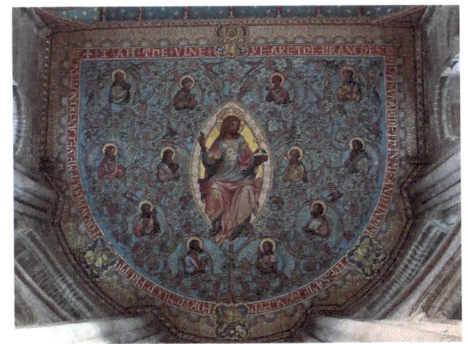

Ceiling above high altar

Ceilings There are two very different ceilings above this area: ribbed ceiling and painted ceiling. The splendid ribbed ceiling covers the area from the east side of the crossing to just before the high altar baldachin. It is late-14th century, but was redone in the late-19th century. This complex ceiling features a design of many squares formed by the ribs. The flat area is rectangular and is painted a pretty greenish-blue, crisscrossed with painted and gilded ribs and bosses. Adding to the visual interest are the floor-to-ceiling shafts. These flare out at clerestory level into ribbed-faceted panels which connect with the vaulting. Each faceted panel is further decorated with portraits inside roundels.

Directly above the high altar, the painted ceiling is amazing, all turquoise, gold, and red, the centerpiece of which is a large portrait of a seated "Christ in Majesty," one hand raised, holding a globe in the other. He is surrounded by depictions of the four Evangelists as well as saints with crowns in their hands.

Mary Queen of Scots Tomb Set into the wall screen on the south side is the memorial to Mary Queen of Scots, who was initially buried here in 1587 after her execution at nearby Fotheringhay Castle. She was later removed to Westminster Abbey in 1612 by her son, James I of England.

➢ *Exit to the new building [Floor Plan #7].*

Fan-vaulted ceiling

NEW BUILDING

This addition is the newest part of the church, built between 1496 and 1509. This space provided a processional route around the east end of the cathedral, linking the north and south choir aisles. Among its several attractions, surely the fan-vaulted ceiling takes first prize.

Fan-vaulted Ceiling The 16th-century fan vaulting was designed by John Wastell, who installed the famous vaulting at King's College Chapel, Cambridge. The fan vaulting here is one of the finest examples in the country.

Hedda Stone Set against the west wall is the Monk's Stone, or Hedda Stone. This evocative carved block of stone dates to the 8th century and is one of the few items remaining from the Saxon Abbey on

Hedda Stone

this site. The piece has an eerie quality, caused by the eyes of the monks which peer out from carved sockets, worn and weathered by time. This remarkable stone is carved on two sides, memorializing the massacre of the Abbot Hedda and his monks a few years before by Danish raiders.

Catherine of Aragon tomb

Windows The new building has many large traceried windows. They are made up of fragments of the original medieval windows smashed by Cromwell's men in 1643.

➢ *Proceed to the north choir aisle [Floor Plan #8].*

NORTH CHOIR AISLE

The two things of special interest along this aisle are Queen Catherine's tomb and the old clock.

Catherine of Aragon's Tomb Queen Catherine died in exile at nearby Kimbolton Castle in 1536. Easily passed by, her tomb consists of a stone cover and a handsome wrought-iron fence, and is decorated with the flags of England and Aragon, Spain. Her tomb plaque is inscribed with "Katharine Queen of England," a title she was denied at the time of her death. The old tomb was destroyed by the Puritans.

Old Clock Further down the choir aisle are the mechanical parts of the old clock. It was said to be the oldest working clock mechanism in the world until 1950 when it was replaced. One part of the mechanism is thought to date back to 1350.

Traces of the old entrance to the now-destroyed 13th-century Lady Chapel may be seen in the north wall of this choir aisle.

➢ *Enter into the main north transept [Floor Plan #9].*

MAIN NORTH TRANSEPT

Like the main south transept, the highlights of this one are the wood ceiling and the Norman architecture. The chapels here are separated by Norman piers, and are surrounded by carved medieval screens, moved here from the nave in the late-18th century. One of these spaces is now occupied by the cathedral's treasury, which has a large collection of silver and other objects of interest.

➢ *Exit via the west front.*

PROFILES OF THE 13 CHURCHES
NORTHEAST

Emperor Constantine, York

Lincoln Cathedral

West front

Personal Impressions

This huge cathedral sits at the top of a hill overlooking the modern city and looms over its surroundings. Its three tall and massive towers can be seen from far away. What a perfect setting for a Gothic cathedral. The area around the cathedral is characterized by narrow, often vertiginous, streets lined with many Tudor and medieval buildings. Today, charming cake shops, cafés, wine stores, and galleries in ancient buildings line the fourth steepest street in England, which connects the cathedral area to the lower town. Although touristy, they are not tacky. Cute private gardens half visible behind the lime-stone walls add to the ambiance.

The stand-out feature of the cathedral for us was its massive, overwhelming west front: an extremely wide screen front (a partial flat façade covered with niches and statuary) topped with two imposing towers. Although the designs are rather different, Lincoln Cathedral shares with Peterborough Cathedral, our award for the most peculiar west front in England. Like them or not, these façades are certainly not boring.

We were especially taken by the two rare and beautiful stained-glass rose windows in the south and north transepts. And, as in a few other English Gothic churches, the ceilings alone are worth the trip.

Among this cathedral's many notable fans is the Victorian writer John Ruskin who declared: "I have always held…that the cathedral of Lincoln is… the most precious piece of architecture in the British Isles and roughly speaking worth any other two cathedrals we have." It's hard to argue.

Either before or after visiting the cathedral, it's worth crossing over to the nearby 11th-century Norman castle, constructed by William the Conqueror. We enjoyed walking around the walls from which there are views of the huge castle complex, the cathedral, the city, and the countryside.

History

Lincoln Cathedral has a commanding view over the countryside and was situated at the convergence of two major Roman roads. Historically, the area suffered from destruction by Viking and other invaders and by domestic events. Realizing the strategic importance of this location, William the Conqueror built the castle and the cathedral here. His immediate motive was to consolidate his power against potential uprisings following his conquest of the country. Building of the cathedral began in 1088, overseen by the first bishop Remigius, and it was consecrated in 1142. Lincoln was destroyed by a massive earthquake in 1185. Only the lower part of the west end and the two attached towers remained. Rebuilding began in 1192 at the east end, this time organized by Bishop Hugh (later St Hugh). The nave was constructed in the Early Gothic style with pointed arches, flying buttresses, and ribbed vaulting. Different parts of the cathedral show the transition from Norman to each subsequent style of English Gothic.

During the Reformation, all the cathedral's treasures were looted. A reforming bishop further desecrated the church, destroying images and monuments, so that by 1548 no sculpture or tomb remained. The Civil War was even worse, when the city was sacked by Cromwell's forces. His soldiers broke the beautiful windows, ripped out the brass memorials, wrecked the bishop's palace, and even threatened to pull down the cathedral itself. None of the old glass has survived in the nave.

In World War II, Lincolnshire was home to many Bomber Command airfields, giving rise to the nickname of Bomber County. The station badge for the nearby RAF Base in Waddington depicts Lincoln Cathedral rising through the clouds. Approximately 55,000 Bomber Command airmen were lost in the war.

Building

The building is cruciform, with one major transept, plus a vestigial transept towards the east end. Although Lincoln looks huge, it is only middle-sized compared with the giants with its total length of 484 feet (148m) and most other dimensions. It is, however, the third largest cathedral in England in floor space, after St Paul's and York. Given the exceptionally chopped up and complicated floor plan, navigating the space can present a challenge to visitors.

Exterior

EXCHEQUER ENTRY GATE

By the 13th century, the cathedral compound was surrounded by a wall and protected by strong gateways. Two of these remain: the "Exchequer Gate," opposite the west end; and the "Potter Gate" on the north flank. Most visitors enter the cathedral grounds from the town through the west gate. Although this ancient gate is not small it is dwarfed by the cathedral looming behind.

WEST FRONT

Arresting features of the massive west front include the unusually wide architectural screen design of this façade, which projects far out from the north and south side walls, and the two huge square towers, both 200 feet (61m) high. The three deep recesses which comprise the central area of the west front are remnants of the earlier Norman church. The arcade of intersecting arches above the two side recesses and the three lower stories of the towers are in the Norman style. The rest of the tall, wide architectural screen is Early Gothic work, erected c.1200–1250. The north and south corners of the screen are topped with pointed turrets. A statue of St Hugh sits atop the south turret.

Note the large 15th-century windows above each of the three west doorways which provide entry into the cathedral. The doorways are deeply recessed

Frieze

and are decorated with geometric shapes, fanciful figures, and beasts. There is a rare display of Norman-era carvings here, especially the band of horizontal friezes which dates from about 1130. The "Gallery of Kings" frieze of royal statues (from William I to Edward III) above the large central door, erected c.1350–1380, stands out.

TOWERS

Central Tower This tower has a history of instability. When the original tower collapsed into the interior of the cathedral in 1237, it was replaced by a new one with a spire that reached a height of 525 feet (160m). This made it the world's tallest structure from 1311 to 1549, surpassing even the Great Pyramid of Giza. Its immense lead-covered timber spire blew down in the mid-16th century. Today, this spire-less tower is still the highest in England at 271 feet (83m). However, given their intact spires, Salisbury and Norwich have central towers which exceed this height. This tower houses five bells including its largest, "The Great Tom of Lincoln," which, recast in 1835, weighs over five tons (4,536 kilos).

West Towers Both of the two west towers are 200 feet (61m) high. Like the central tower, each has many arcaded openings, four pinnacles, and a decorative screen at the top. Each has a large attached buttress at all four corners. The southwest tower houses 13 bells, while the northwest tower has only two.

JUDGMENT PORCH

At the east end of the cathedral's south wall is the southeast porch—aka The Judgment Porch. This unusual and lovely external entrance to the Angel Choir is worthy of note for its superbly detailed carving. Influenced by the French Gothic style, above the double doors is a tympanum with a central figure of Christ set in a quatrefoil. He is flanked by carved angels, as well as souls rising to Heaven or being dragged down to Hell by demons. This portal also features a statue of the Virgin Mary between the double doors. Just beside the porch are carvings of a king and queen, thought to be either Edward I and Eleanor of

Castile, or Margaret of Valois, his second wife. Some of the sculpture is 19th century.

CHAPTER HOUSE BUTTRESSING

Externally, at the northeast corner of the cathedral, there is a remarkable array of flying buttresses that spring inward from stubby buttress piers, then attach themselves to the chapter house walls. Thick, heavy buttress piers support the eight free-standing flying buttresses.

➢ *Enter via the west front [Floor Plan #1].*

Interior

The ceilings are worth the trip to Lincoln—they are imaginative and entertaining. There are several different ceiling and rib designs throughout the building, and each area of the cathedral can be identified solely by its unique vaulted ceiling.

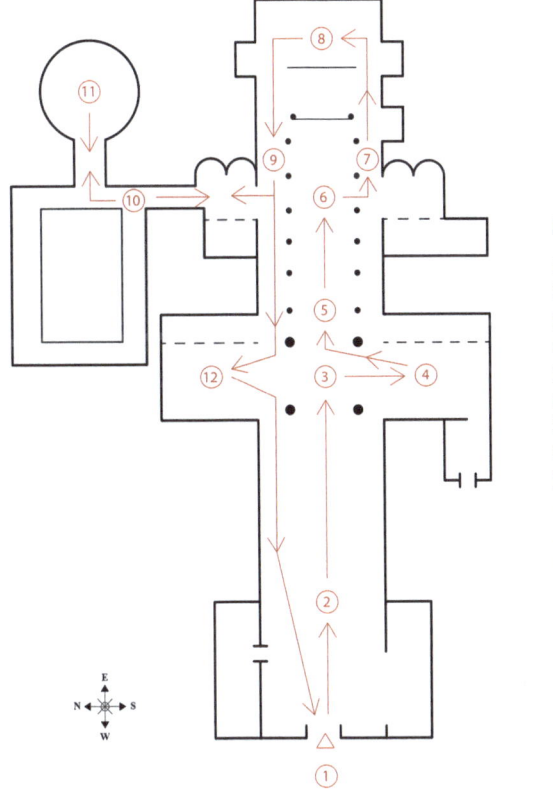

Floor Plan

1. West front
2. Nave
3. Crossing
4. Southwest transept
5. Choir area
6. High altar area
7. South choir aisle
8. Angel Choir
9. North choir aisle
10. Cloister
11. Chapter house
12. Northwest transept

Nave looking east

➢ *Proceed to the nave [Floor Plan #2].*

NAVE

The very long 252 feet (77m) nave is mid-13th-century Early Gothic. Each pier is surrounded by eight circular shafts of Purbeck marble. The piers display three different patterns. The moldings of the arcade arches are deeply cut, and there are two lancet windows in each bay of the outer aisles. The vault ribs spring from each side wall via the bundle of shafts that rise from the triforium level to meet the ceiling.

Windows Few windows in the nave are noteworthy, as most original glass was destroyed during the Civil War. One of the few is the handsome stained-glass west window which has five panels in the central row depicting five standing kings, with only the heads of five more nobles in the row below. The window is topped with a number of tracery openings, mainly done in red glass. The window was largely filled with modern glass in the 19th century.

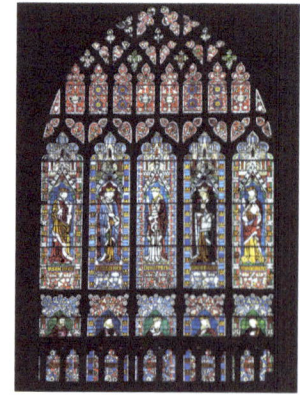
West window

Just above this window is one of Lincoln's four rose windows—perhaps the most in any English Gothic church. The design of this 19th-century rose window depicts the first bishop, a red-robed St Remigius, at the center, surrounded by five roundels.

The windows of the clerestory are plain. All the windows in the aisles are colored, but modern. There are three lancet windows above each main triforium arch in the clerestory level. The triforium design is handsome with its single central pillar and side pillars, surmounted by a carved arch pierced with a quatrefoil opening.

Font At the west end of the nave is a fine example of a Norman-period font. It is made of rare Tournai marble, square in shape, set atop four black stone piers. All four sides are decorated with low relief carvings of mythical beasts.

Mary Magdalene Chapel (aka Morning Chapel) This simple chapel used for quiet prayer is at the northwest end of the nave. It has quatrefoil wall openings which open to the nave, blind arcading, and a central pillar which supports the vaulted ceiling.

Bell Ringer's Chapel The chapel on the southwest corner is now used by the team of church bell ringers. See the unusual 17th-century painted list of the "Names of the Companie of Ringers of Our Blessed Virgen Marie of Lincoln."

➢ *Proceed to the crossing [Floor Plan #3].*

CROSSING

Here at the crossing, the ceiling of the central lantern tower is splendidly decorated with 14th-century ribbed vaulting. The ribs are shaped like a curious eight-pointed star with the ribs forming a square shape in the center. The opening is surrounded on its four sides with two levels of arches, some with windows.

➢ *Enter the southwest transept [Floor Plan #4].*

SOUTHWEST TRANSEPT

The dominant feature here is the mid-14th-century Bishop's Eye window. This window is one of the largest examples of the Decorated style with curvilinear tracery. Due to the small spaces within each tracery panel, there is little iconography within the window. The east wall of this transept houses three un-named chapels; it has a beautiful carved stone

Bishop's Eye window

LINCOLN CATHEDRAL

and wood screen. The north and south transepts are fitted with simple ribbed vaulting.

➢ *Enter the choir area [Floor Plan #5].*

CHOIR AREA

Choir Screen The early-14th-century carved-stone choir screen is Decorated work at its best. Flanking the central opening are four tall, highly decorated niches separated by vertical buttresses crowned with pointed gables. The decoration in the arch moldings alongside the doorway includes flowers, leaves, and animals. Some are backlit to show the perfection of the carving. Looking up and into each gable reveals an elegant ribbed design.

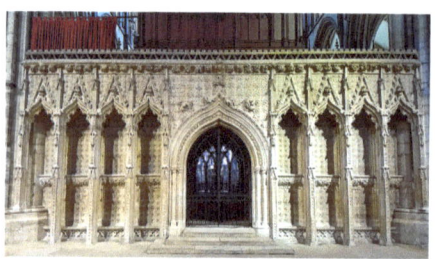
Choir screen

Organ This dramatic organ sits on top of the choir screen. Although the choir screen is not petite, the organ seems even larger by comparison. The organ case is handsome dark wood, topped with three dramatic spires. Indeed, the use of spires characterizes the entire choir area, including the canopies over the choir stalls, and even the pulpit and the Bishop's Throne. William Byrd, the famous Renaissance composer, was the organist here from 1563, using an earlier instrument. The current organ dates only from 1898. It has had two restorations, in 1960 and 1998.

Choir and organ

Choir Entering the choir, we see the earliest known example of pure Early Gothic, with no trace of Norman influence. A number of parishioners were killed here when the central tower fell in 1237. Stone screens behind the stalls, partly erected to strengthen the building, divide the choir from the aisles. The choir stalls were installed in 1370. The brass lectern is dated 1667. There is carving throughout, especially on the misericords.

Bishop's Throne At the southeast end of the choir stalls is the extravagant dark wood 18th-century bishop's throne. The design is all busy Gothic verticality, the seat flanked by two carved architectural columns, and topped with a tall, spiky pinnacle.

Pulpit The pulpit sits across the aisle from the bishop's throne, perched on a delicate-looking carved white stone base. Designed by George Scott and installed in 1863, it has a heavily carved dark-wood top with an elaborate spire.

Ceiling A series of asymmetrical vaults with two ribs on one side connects to only a single rib on the other side of the vault. Wags refer to this design as "crazy vaulting."

➢ *Continue to the high altar area [Floor Plan #6].*

HIGH ALTAR AREA

The principal item of interest here is the high altar screen, which was restored in the middle of the 18th century, but retains some 13th-century work. The design is tall open-work, made from carved white stone. It has a tall gable in the center with pinnacles on each side. The screen is backed with a low, carved solid "wall" that spans the room. The large east window looms behind.

The vaulting consists of ribbed triangles which spring from clustered wall-mounted shafts. The two other interesting features of this area include:

Easter Sepulcher Tomb Near the high altar on the north side is this late-13th-century tomb. It is a fine piece of stone carving in the Decorated style in the form of six slender canopies. Note the carvings of three sleeping soldiers on the lower right-hand panels.

Burial Monument of Katherine Swynford On the south side is this monument. Swynford was the 14th-century governess of John of Gaunt's children, then his mistress, and finally his wife and mother of four of his children. John of Gaunt was a son of Edward III of England, and it was through this royal Swynford ancestry that Henry VII claimed the throne of England. Her tomb consists of a simple painted wood casket with a beautiful, carved stone arch over the top.

➢ *Enter the south choir aisle [Floor Plan #6].*

SOUTH CHOIR AISLE

This aisle is separated from the choir by a carved stone screen. The highlights in this section include the remnants of the shrine of Little St Hugh and the Apprentice Wall.

Shrine of Little St Hugh Legend has it that in the 13th century the body of a missing boy was found in a well. This incident became the source of a blood libel, with Jews accused of his abduction, torture, and murder. Many Jews were arrested and 18 were hanged. The boy was then dubbed "Little St Hugh" to distinguish him from the cathedral's patron, St Hugh. The cathedral benefited because Little Hugh became a martyr, and his shrine became a pilgrim magnet. Chaucer mentions the case in *The Prioress's Tale*. The shrine was mutilated by soldiers in the Civil War.

Apprentice Wall Nearby is the easy-to-miss 'Apprentice Wall' where apprentice masons practiced their art before moving to more challenging assignments. It's interesting to compare these carvings with those on the choir screen which show the work of accomplished masons.

➢ *Proceed to the Angel Choir [Floor Plan #8].*

Angel Choir

ANGEL CHOIR

The Angel Choir (1256–1280) was built when the Early Gothic style was evolving into the Decorated. It is named for the 28 angels which decorate the triforium, some holding musical instruments. The piers consist of clustered shafts with carved capitals of Purbeck marble. The ceiling bosses are considered by some to be England's best.

Entering the Angel Choir from the south aisle, one passes the following:

Russell and Longland Chapels There are two chapels on each side of the Judgment Porch door: The Russell chapel has modern murals on the wall and ceiling. The design of the Longland chapel is more elaborate.

Artist's Monument The monument at the southeast corner of the choir is that of a 19th-century artist.

Shrine of Eleanor of Castile, the Wife of Edward I This handsome tomb is carved from white stone and is emblazoned with coats of arms. Eleanor's Victorian-era bronze effigy lies on top. It is said that this tomb contains only her entrails, and that her heart was buried elsewhere.

East Window The fine 19th-century east window, with its eight narrow panels, is topped with a cluster of Decorated tracery. The dominant color is a striking dark blue. It may be the best example of the Geometrical style—one of two types of Decorated—in England. It measures about 59 feet (18m) by 29 feet (9m). The windows that flank this east window are filled with Early Gothic glass.

St Hugh's Shrine Towards the north corner is the tomb complex of St Hugh, the cathedral's patron. Previously, a number of other shrines and monuments had been here but were destroyed during the Reformation or the Civil War.

Lincoln Imp One of the stone carvings high up on a pier on the north side of the Angel Choir is the so-called 'Lincoln Imp.' According to a 14th-century legend, two mischievous imps were sent by Satan to do evil on Earth. The two imps headed to Lincoln Cathedral, where they smashed tables and chairs and tripped the bishop. When an angel ordered them to stop, one of the imps sat atop a stone pillar and threw rocks at the angel. The angel turned this imp to stone, but the second imp escaped. For the visitors, a console on the floor lights up the small and high-up Imp on demand.

Lincoln Imp

➢ *Enter the north choir aisle [Floor Plan #9].*

NORTH CHOIR AISLE

In about the center of this aisle, note on the left, spanning the arched entry from this aisle into the high altar area, a decorated walkway at the triforium level. In addition to its walkway function, it probably served as a brace to strengthen this area structurally.

Decorated walkway brace

➢ *Turn into the passageway leading to the cloister [Floor Plan #10].*

CLOISTER

The late-13th-century cloister is on the north side of the cathedral. Since Lincoln was non-monastic, the cloister here is small. The ceiling is unpainted wood

Wooden ceiling

with eight-part ribbed vaults. Note that the cloister ceiling repeats the unusual crazy-vaulting design. Many carved wood bosses decorate each rib intersection. The wood ribs spring from the spandrels between the series of heavily molded white stone arches. The walkways are lined with plain glass windows. The beauty is in the elegant tracery design of the stone window frames, which support the quatrefoil and large roundel opening at the top.

MEDIEVAL LIBRARY AND WREN LIBRARY

Virtually hidden above the north-side walkway of the cloister, the Medieval Library (built in 1422) and the Wren Library (1676) are accessed via a flight of fine wooden stairs. They are in the timber-framed building with a magnificently decorated roof and furnished with oak reading desks. These libraries hold many ancient books and precious manuscripts: a letter of Edward I and a large collection of printed work, including a copy of the 1106 Vulgate Bible.

➢ *Proceed to the chapter house [Floor Plan #11].*

CHAPTER HOUSE

This beautiful chapter house is Early Gothic, completed about 1230. It has an unusual ten sides, with a diameter of 59 feet (18m); a quatrefoil frieze; and a pyramidal roof. There is an ancient "official" chair here, which is said to have been the throne of Edward I when he held his Parliament in this room. Other features include:

Ceiling The passage into the chapter house has blind arcading and a molded doorway. The dramatic star-vaulted wooden ceiling inside is held up by a central pillar with attached Purbeck marble shafts, and a vault with molded ribs and bosses.

Windows The lancet windows on the side walls are filled with modern glass. An arcade runs around the walls beneath the windows. Above the entrance is yet another rose window whose design begins with an inner circle with two outer circles. The entire window is decorated with red and blue glass, against a busy, light background.

➢ *Continue to the northwest transept [Floor Plan #12].*

NORTHWEST TRANSEPT

The most important feature of this transept is its huge stained-glass rose window, called the "Dean's Eye Window." This early-13th-century window depicts the story of the Last Judgment and faces north, where evil was believed to come from. About 70 percent of the glass is original.

Dean's Eye window

There are several chapels on the east wall of this transept, dedicated to Sts Michael, Andrew, and George. These chapels are memorials for soldiers, sailors, and airmen who died in wars across the globe and over the centuries.

➢ *Return to nave and exit via portal on west front.*

York Minster

West front

Personal Impressions

Entering the old city through the 4th-century gate and crossing the bridge over the Ouse River inside the city gives one a wonderful feeling of history. York Minster is set on an elevated site where it can be viewed from many vantage points. The town is full of interesting streets, buildings, and monuments—a mix of old and new—still surrounded by the ancient city wall.

This huge minster fits right into this bustling town, conveying a sense of grandeur and taste, inside and outside. We were especially taken with the west front, an elegant and balanced façade.

The inside is so wide that we felt almost lost. The central wooden ceiling with bosses was elegant but not as elaborate or wild as in some other churches. The most noticeable feature was the 128 medieval glass—stained, painted, and enameled—windows. They are beautiful, although it is hard to differentiate the original ones from the rehabilitated ones. The polygonal chapter house was handsome with an interesting ceiling and intricate floor tiles. Without doubt the most remarkable feature here at York is the huge 15th-century stained-glass east window. The largest expanse of medieval glass in the world, it is said to be the size of a tennis court.

After checking every detail inside the cathedral, we moved outside and enjoyed the grassy, tree-filled, Dean's Park on the north side of the cathedral. One can spend hours sitting there admiring the cathedral with fellow visitors.

History

York Minster is the seat of the Archbishop of York who is second only to the Archbishop of Canterbury in the Church of England. He leads the Church's Northern Province. Though a cathedral, York is always referred to as minster. The title "minster" derives originally from an Anglo-Saxon missionary teaching church, but became an honorific title given to certain churches. Services in the church are on the High Church or Anglo-Catholic end of the Anglican continuum.

In 306 CE, the Roman general Constantine was proclaimed emperor by his troops here in the Roman basilica, which is now under the south transept. His statue sits outside alongside the south wall. Several churches were built on this site beginning 627 CE. The attached school and library were considered among the best in Northern Europe by the 8th century. The Danes destroyed the existing church in 1075, but it was rebuilt around 1080 in the Norman style. Although construction of the present building began in 1220, it was not consecrated until 1472. The choir and crypt were remodeled in 1154, and a new chapel was built all in the Norman style. Soon after, the Early Gothic style arrived in England via Canterbury. A major motivation for subsequent renovations and rebuilding was the desire to keep up with the evolving Gothic design. Another was simply to replace and repair damage due to fires and collapsing towers.

Due to the fighting between the Scots and the English in the 13th century, Edward I made York his main city in the north. That made York extremely prosperous, which helped generate the funding needed to build the costly cathedral.

Henry VIII's Reformation resulted in the looting of much of the cathedral's treasures and the loss of much of its lands. Elizabeth I followed this with the destruction of tombs, windows, and altars. During the Civil War, the city fell to Cromwell, but Lord Thomas Fairfax prevented his Puritan forces from damaging the cathedral.

The cathedral has been damaged by fires many times over the centuries. These included arson attacks and lightning fires. A 1984 lightning fire cracked the rose window in the south transept into 40 thousand pieces and destroyed the south transept roof.

During both World Wars most of the windows were removed, then pieced back together after the wars. Cathedral records show that much of the plain replacement glass came from Germany. York artisans painted and fired the plain glass, then reconstructed the windows using lead strips. Their appearance varies due to the different types of glazing and painting techniques used over hundreds of years.

Building

York Minster is one of the largest cathedrals in Northern Europe. It is exceptionally long at 525 feet (160m). It also has the biggest chapter house, and the finest windows in England. Some of the stained glass dates back to the 12th century. Approximately two million individual pieces of glass make up the cathedral's 128 stained-glass windows. It has more historic stained glass than any other buildings in the UK, a remarkable 60 percent of all surviving medieval stained glass.

Since it was never a monastic church it has no cloister, although it does have a chapter house. Made of creamy-white limestone, the cathedral is a showcase of the evolution of English Gothic architecture from Early Gothic to the Perpendicular style.

The floor plan conforms to the common, single transept, cruciform design. Other distinctive features are the undercroft and crypt below the floor.

Exterior

WEST FRONT

To our taste this west front is one of the best. It is majestic and harmonious without excess despite its various styles. Numerous niches cover the surface of the west front. It is doubtful whether they ever contained statues. Tall towers, each with its own two deeply recessed windows, flank the central section, which is dominated by the large, gable-topped west window. Thanks to the heart design of its upper tracery and its popularity, it is affectionately known as the Heart of Yorkshire. Below this window is the simple but elegant center portal with its own gable.

TOWERS AND BELLS

There are three towers: two western and one central.

Western Towers Erected from 1433 to 1472, the two western towers are heavily decorated and are capped with pinnacles. Between them, these towers have a total of 56 bells, the largest number of bells in any English church. These bells are regarded as masterpieces.

The northwest tower houses the so-called 'Great Peter Bell,' which weighs 24,192 lbs (12 tons) and strikes on the hour. It is the largest bell in England.

A fire in 1840 wrecked the nave and south aisle of the interior as well as the southwest tower. Restoration of the damage was done in 1858. This tower holds two kinds of bells. a) The 14 main "peal bells" are hung in a frame and are attached to wheels which turn through 360 degrees allowing the English form of change ringing to take place. b) The 22 carillon bells are played from a keyboard in the ringing chamber below. This permits tunes to be chimed. In 2008 York Minster became the first cathedral in England to have a carillon of bells.

Central Tower This very large but rather plain structure is a lantern tower with two windows on each of its four sides. There are no bells in this tower. A pair of narrow, attached buttresses supports each angle of the tower. The 275 narrow steps lead to the top, which offers a great view of the town and surrounding countryside. Like several other English Gothic churches, York has shallow foundations—those here are only five feet (1.5m) deep. This may account for the collapse of the central tower in the early-15th century; it was soon replaced. Even then, continuing concerns about the tower's stability led to the reinforcement of the four main supporting piers with massive concrete collars at their base. These reinforcements can be seen in the crypt.

CHAPTER HOUSE EXTERIOR

This practically detached octagonal structure is located adjacent to the north transept façade. It has a very high pyramidal roof and six large free-standing buttresses which connect with the walls at the corner of each facet via flying buttresses.

Interior

➢ *Enter via the left portal on the west front [Floor Plan # 1] into the nave [Floor Plan #2].*

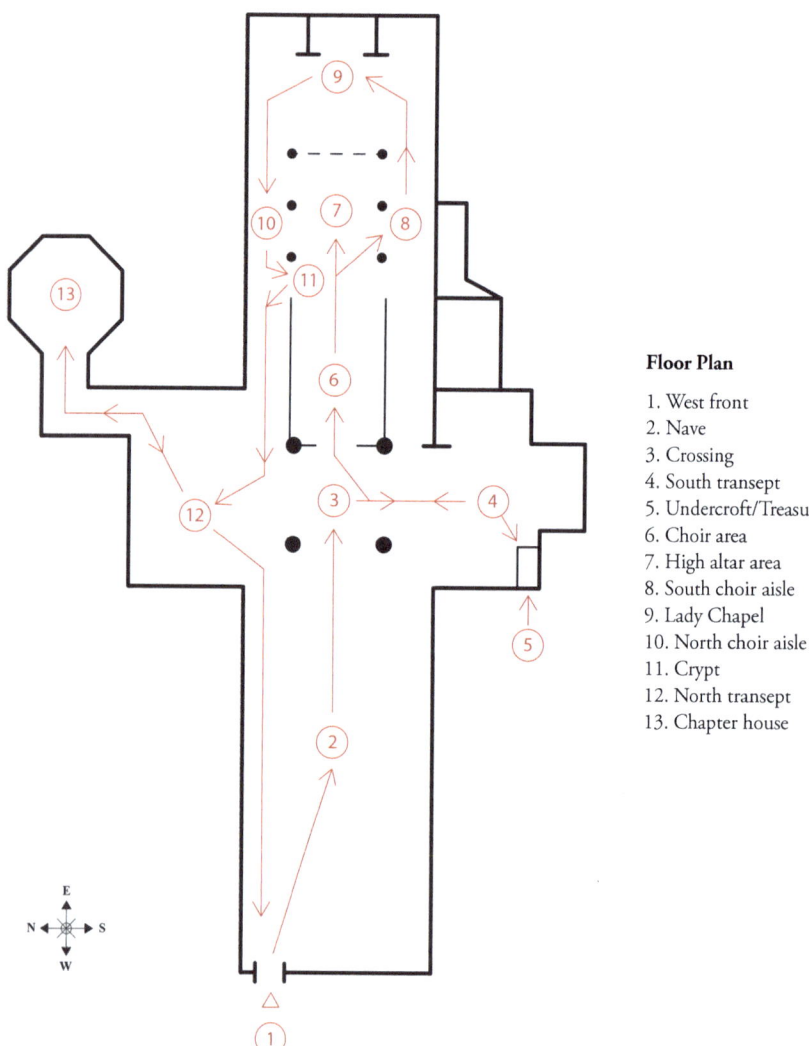

Floor Plan

1. West front
2. Nave
3. Crossing
4. South transept
5. Undercroft/Treasury
6. Choir area
7. High altar area
8. South choir aisle
9. Lady Chapel
10. North choir aisle
11. Crypt
12. North transept
13. Chapter house

NAVE

Standing in the wide 14th-century Decorated-style nave gives one a sense of the great size of the cathedral. Contributing to this impression is that York has one of the higher vaults in England at 95 feet (29m) in the nave and 102 feet (31m) in the choir. The tall arcade arches reach more than halfway to the ceiling, resulting in a small triforium to make room for larger windows at the clerestory level. The piers with attached shafts have

Nave and west window

octagonal bases. The capitals are gilded and are beautifully carved with foliage—sometimes a figure can be seen amidst the foliage. Coats of arms of the benefactors of York appear on each side of the main arches.

Ceiling Given the great width of the nave, the builders substituted a wooden ceiling for a stone one since this reduced the need for supportive buttressing. The fact that this lovely ceiling is made of wood, painted white with gold highlights, is not obvious. The shafts ascend from the floor to the clerestory level, where they divide into the ribs that form the ribbed ceiling. It seems that every intersection of the ribs is fitted with a gilded boss, representing various biblical themes. This ceiling is a replica of the old ceiling destroyed by the 1840 fire.

Great West Window This mid-14th-century window—the Heart of Yorkshire—features the flowing tracery of the later Decorated period. It is composed of eight slender lancets. It is one of the finest medieval windows in England. Niches and arcading cover the wall alongside and below the window.

Wooden Dragon Projecting from the triforium on the north side of the nave is a curious gilded wooden dragon, which it is believed used to hold the rope which raised the former font cover. There is currently no permanent font under it.

Gilded wooden dragon

➢ *Proceed to the crossing [Floor Plan #3].*

CROSSING

The square ceiling of the lantern tower above the crossing is constructed in a crisscross of elegant ribbing. The design is a matrix of squares and triangles against a white background. Each intersection is fitted with a gilded boss. Four simple fans of ribs spring from the single shafts on each side and at each corner. There are two windows on each of its side walls.

➢ *Proceed to the south transept [Floor Plan #4].*

SOUTH TRANSEPT

This 13th-century transept is of Early Gothic design. Note that this transept triforium is not minimized; it is larger than in the nave, whereas the clerestory is smaller.

Rose Window Dating from about 1500, this large rose window is the most important feature of this transept. It commemorates the union of the royal houses of York and Lancaster. Below are lancet windows with old glass.

Ceiling The 15th-century ceilings of the south and north transepts are made of wood. These barrel-shaped ceilings are covered with a network of ribbing painted a contrasting white. The south transept ceiling burned in 1984 and was replaced with one with a design similar to the north transept ceiling.

Chapels The two significant chapels here are those of the 13th-century archbishop, Walter de Gray, and St George's, respectively on the east and west walls.

➢ *Go down to the undercroft and treasury [Floor Plan #5].*

UNDERCROFT AND TREASURY

This large underground complex is comprised of multiple chambers featuring archaeology and artifacts going back 2,000 years. Among the holdings are the 1,000-year old "Horn of Ulf" and the "York Gospels" of similar antiquity.

➢ *Enter the choir area [Floor Plan #6].*

CHOIR AREA

Choir Screen Below the central tower crossing is the striking, carved stone choir screen. It is known as the "King's Screen" due to its 15 near life-sized

Choir screen   Choir screen entry

images of kings, from William the Conqueror to Henry VI, all but one carved towards the end of the 15th century.

A special treat awaits those who pass through this choir screen. The doorway itself and the interior passage are brightly painted in red, blue, green, and gold. It is believed that originally other parts of the cathedral were also highly painted.

Organ This organ which sits atop the choir screen is early-19th century, destroyed by fire and replaced soon after. It has been reconstructed several times. It is a large, dramatic instrument, decorated with tall pinnacles on each side and shorter ones across the top. The case is surrounded by gilded and painted pipes.

Choir Stalls The Perpendicular-design choir was erected early in the 15th century. This is one of the most aesthetic choirs in England. An early-19th-century fire destroyed all the old carved stalls and misericords. Fortunately, the modern substitutes are decent reproductions.

Archbishop's Throne At the east end of the choir stalls, the Archbishop's throne is an extravaganza in heavily carved dark oak. Like similar thrones in other cathedrals, a very tall Gothic canopy towers above it. Perhaps unique to York Minster, there are two apparently identical bishop's thrones across the central choir aisle from each other.

Ceiling above Choir and High Altar Areas This complicated ceiling is made of wood, like that in the nave. It is decorated with many foliated bosses.

➤ *Enter the high altar area [Floor Plan #7].*

High altar screen

HIGH ALTAR AREA

The high altar is made of carved wood, with a tall backdrop of dramatic red velvet. Behind the high altar is a tall, wide altar screen. It is a reproduction of the ancient one, carved from white stone with a square design. Seven piers support a carved flat-topped plinth which spans the area from north to south. Between each pier is a lancet design of carved open work, showing the great east window behind.

➢ *Proceed to south choir aisle [Floor Plan #8] and enter Lady Chapel [Floor Plan #9].*

LADY CHAPEL

The Lady Chapel, dating from the last half of the 14th century, occupies the four east bays. The highlights of this area are the great east window and the fine altar screen below it.

Great East Window At the east end of the Lady Chapel is the remarkable early-15th-century window. Restored in early 2018, this 600-year-old great east window depicts the beginning and end of all things from the Book of Genesis to the Book of Revelation. Although it is surpassed in size by the great east window at Gloucester Cathedral, this window has more old glass: 117 glass panels in 13 rows of nine each, and 144 tracery compartments. It is 78 feet (24m) high. Across the bottom row are depictions of kings and bishops: some of the best glass portraits from England's Middle Ages.

In the space in front of this window there is a steel dome containing five of the conserved panels from the window. This orb was set up in 2012. Viewing it up close reveals the outstanding detail in each panel. The orb enables visitors to see the work of renowned medieval glass artist John Thornton.

Altar Screen Below the window is a 1923 carved and colored screen, dedicated to Queen Victoria. The focus of the screen is a three-panel nativity scene with the Magi and shepherds.

St Stephen's Chapel This chapel is at the northeast corner of the Lady Chapel. Its major feature is the terracotta panel called "The First Hour of the Crucifixion," added in 1937.

➢ *Enter the north choir aisle [Floor Plan #10], and take the stairs into the crypt [Floor Plan #11].*

CRYPT

Stairways leading down to the crypt are on each side of aisles that run alongside the choir and high altar. Although the crypt is below ground, there is no access between it and the Undercroft–Treasury. This large crypt was discovered only in the 19th century. The Norman piers feature herring-bone carving from the Old Saxon church and elaborate figurative carvings on the capitals. The most dramatic of these is the so-called 'Doomstone' capital depicting sinners headed for Hell. In addition, there are some interesting antiquities, such as ancient wall murals, statuary, and an Anglo-Saxon stone plaque from 800 CE which has an ornamented cross with swirling vine decorations. The cathedral's only historic font, which depicts the baptism of King Edwin, is also here.

York was forced to compete for pilgrims and donations after Thomas Becket was buried at Canterbury. It soon had its own saint: St William of York. While his remains are behind the

Doomstone

Ancient mural

high altar, his shrine is set on a platform on top of the arches of the crypt. Edward I and bishops carried his relics to their new resting-place.

➢ *Go to the north transept [Floor Plan #12].*

NORTH TRANSEPT

This transept is in the Early Gothic style and resembles the south transept, but differs in details. The highlights include the Five Sisters Window, the astronomical clock, and two chapels.

Five Sisters Window The major feature here is the Five Sisters window (c.1250), consisting of five gray-green glass windows, surmounted by five small lancet windows in the gable. Over 100,000 pieces of glass are set into a series of complex geometric designs and incorporated colored glass. The five main panels are the largest ancient lancets in England at 52 feet (16m) high. While these windows are large and impressive, the glass is somber with little visible figuration.

Five Sisters window

Astronomical Clock The lovely clock was installed in this transept in the mid-20th century as a memorial to wartime aircrews. The dial shows the locations of the sun in relation to York and certain navigational stars important to the aircrews. The clock entertains visitors with statues of two knights below the dial who wield hammers to strike a metal bar at regular intervals.

Chapels The two notable chapels are: the St John chapel, which is a memorial to the airmen who died during World War II, and the Military Women's chapel on the east wall, which is dedicated to Britain's military women who died in World War I.

➢ *Proceed to the chapter house [Floor Plan #13].*

CHAPTER HOUSE

The Decorated-style chapter house is reached via the north transept. It is the largest and is easily one of the finest in England. Note the following:

Chapter house

Ceiling Despite a span of 58 feet (18m), the 13th-century wooden roof has no central support. It is held up with a network of beams. The rounded central ceiling's beautiful ribs meet at the central boss. The spaces between the ribs are delicately painted with floral designs.

Windows The seven large traceried stained-glass windows cover almost all of the upper wall space, filling the chapter house with light. The many window panels depict the Passion as well as many saints.

Stone Stalls and Canopies Each stall is flanked by free-standing Purbeck shafts which rise up to meet the heavily carved marble canopy. The carved stonework is exceptional, depicting images of mice, cats, dogs, a jester, pigs, squirrels feeding on acorns, men gathering grapes, birds, coiled dragons, and reptiles. The gallery of medieval faces portraying all manner of curious and interesting expressions.

➢ *Exit via the cathedral shop.*

Durham Cathedral

Three-quarter view

Personal Impressions

Built to the same size and scale as the old St Peters in Rome, Durham Cathedral is located at the northeast corner of England, near the Scottish border. The cathedral can be reached from the city center or from many of the woodland footpaths and walks along the riverbanks. The walk up to the cathedral through the town takes visitors via a maze of old streets and buildings. Being a university town, Durham is crowded with young people and has lots of lively cafés.

We were attracted to this cathedral by its reputation not simply as the largest but as the most perfect monument of Norman style architecture in England. The overall impression of the cathedral, especially from the outside, is stern and commanding due to its origins, brownish stone, sheer mass, and relative lack of decoration. Yet, despite its somber gravitas, the cathedral has many fine features.

Since the cathedral occupies a dramatic position on a promontory high above the River Wear, placing the west front, Galilee Chapel, and towers at the edge of a deep gorge, one can only view the cathedral from the sides and back. Perhaps the best views of the west front can be had from the other side of the river.

Inside the cathedral, our first impression was how dark it was. The low illumination results in part from its drum piers (massive circular versions of piers), unglazed triforium, and smallish clerestory windows. These unique cylindrical piers with their chevron zigzag patterns in the nave give visitors a sense of the Norman architecture that preceded Gothic. They also give visitors an idea of what the cathedral looked like in the old days.

History

Legend has it that itinerant monks settled in Durham thanks to a cow. According to the story, in 995 CE the monks of Lindisfarne were seeking refuge from marauding Danes. They were carrying the coffin of their patron St Cuthbert, which suddenly became too heavy to carry. At that point, they spotted a "dun-colored" (i.e., tan-colored) cow standing on a rocky outcrop overlooking the River Wear, and took it as a sign from the saint that they should build a church on this spot.

Construction on the new cathedral began in 1093 at the eastern end, the basic structure largely completed in only 40 years. The resources to build and renovate were provided by the bishops and monks from their large revenues. Major additions and renovations were made over the years, but most of it remains essentially Norman in design. Oddly enough, the entire exterior of the cathedral was originally whitewashed.

Cuthbert's tomb was destroyed by order of Henry VIII in 1538. Most of the cathedral's treasures were also destroyed or appropriated. Cuthbert's body was exhumed and reburied under a plain stone slab. His new and simple shrine is one of the centerpieces of the cathedral.

Given Durham's proximity to the unsettled Scottish border, from the 11th to the 19th centuries, its prince–bishop, appointed by William the Conqueror, had both military and religious power over the area. A mark of this bishop's status is that he stands at the right hand of the monarch at coronations even today.

After the Battle of Dunbar in 1650, Oliver Cromwell used the cathedral to imprison several thousand Scottish prisoners of war. Kept largely without food, water, or heat, some 1,700 died. The prisoners destroyed much of the cathedral woodwork to use for firewood. It is believed that the dead were buried in unmarked graves, while the survivors were shipped as slave labor to North America.

Building

While the building is essentially Norman, the cathedral was one of the first in Europe to utilize all three essential elements of Gothic architecture: pointed arches, ribbed vaults, and flying buttresses. Although Norman builders generally used round arches, these evolved over time into slightly pointed ones. The nave aisles and choir (c.1104) are supported by the first known examples of pointed ribbed vaults. They cross at the top and shift the weight of the building to the buttresses and vertical shafts which rise to support the ceiling ribs.

Another innovation was to employ piers, with attached shafts, which alternate with the simpler Norman drum piers. Essential to building stability, but unseen, are the flying buttresses concealed within the triforium.

These changes are believed to precede the Gothic architecture of France by a few decades. This remarkable development is no doubt due to the Norman stonemasons who constructed this basically Norman-style building.

This is a huge building with an overall length of 470 feet (143m) with a nave over 200 feet (61m) long and 81 feet (25m) wide. The low nave ceiling—at 72 feet (22m)—demonstrates the English emphasis on length over height. Except for the large Galilee Chapel at the west front, the floor plan is conventional, with a single transept. An important feature is the large east end, which is much wider than the exterior walls of the choir and high altar area.

Exterior

WEST FRONT

The appearance of the west front is a bit mysterious because, given its position at the edge of a cliff, the only view one can get of it is from a distance, and even this is partially blocked by trees. The main features of this front are the tall, closely spaced, square west towers topped with pinnacles, and the Galilee Chapel which juts out from the lower part of the west front. Above the chapel is the large west window inserted about 1346. This pointed window is surrounded by a stone arch, which in turn is surmounted by a small gable.

NORTH DOOR

The entrance to the cathedral is via this door. The columns on each side of the door have carved capitals, and the arch molding is richly ornamented with chevrons, foliage, and lozenges, plus some curious carvings. Note the historical bronze door knocker. In the Middle Ages churches gave refuge to lawbreakers who came to secure sanctuary from mob violence or secular law. Two porters watched for fugitives, and when a refuge-seeker knocked he was admitted and given shelter for up to 37 days. The earliest known instance of persons claiming protection was about 740 CE, and the last in 1623. The current doorknocker is a replica of the 12th-century original, which is displayed in the Cathedral Treasures exhibit inside the building.

Sanctuary door knocker

TOWERS
There are three towers: two at the west front and a central lantern tower.

Western Towers Dating from the 12th and 13th centuries, these towers are square and solid, but are leavened with pinnacles. The upper area consists of four levels. These towers are mainly of Norman design up to the level of the nave roof. The upper portion was added in the 13th century, and the present pinnacles and open parapets were added at the end of the 18th century. Originally the towers had tall wooden spires covered with lead. These were removed in the middle of the 17th century.

Central Lantern Tower This huge central tower dates from the 15th century. It is the oldest and largest of the towers, but lacks ornamentation. Given its height of 217 feet (66m) and its position atop a hill, it can be seen from a great distance. The upper level has twin two-pane windows on each face. The very top is surmounted by a deep open-work parapet. Each corner of the tower is fitted with two top-to-bottom attached buttresses, decorated with niches containing figures. It was damaged by lightning and replaced twice in the 15th century. The current tower was restored in the mid-19th century.

Belfry and Bells The belfry at the top of the central tower contains eight bells. The bell-ringer's gallery sits just above the tower crossing ceiling.

Dun Cow Sculpture The 1775 wall relief sculpture depicting the Dun Cow legend is located high on the outside north wall at the north angle of the Nine Altars area.

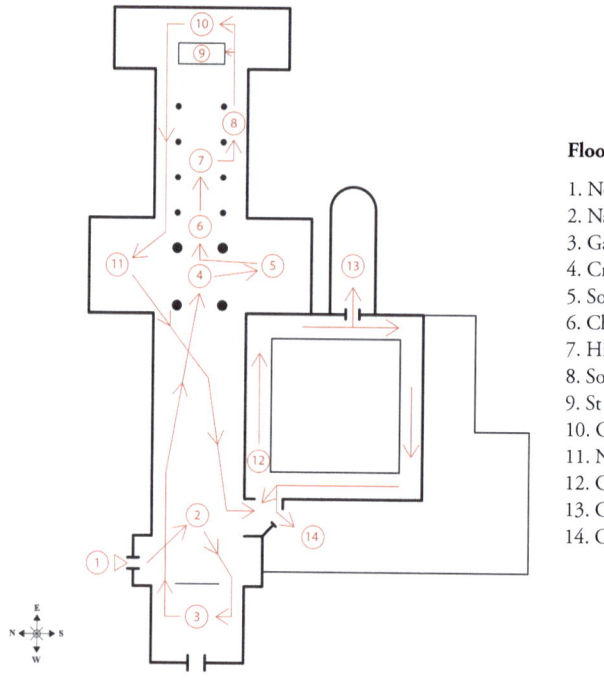

Floor Plan

1. North door entrance
2. Nave
3. Galilee Chapel
4. Crossing
5. South transept
6. Choir area
7. High altar area
8. South choir aisle
9. St Cuthbert shrine
10. Chapel of Nine Altars
11. North transept
12. Cloister
13. Chapter house
14. Open Treasure Gallery

Interior

➢ *Via the north door [Floor Plan #1], enter the nave [Floor Plan #2].*

NAVE

This nave is considered one of the great works of 11th-century Norman architecture. The view from inside the west door reveals the interior panorama. Grand Norman cylindrical drum piers, 23 feet (7m) in circumference, play a major visual role in the nave.

Piers and Arches The nave has the usual three-part elevation: arcade, triforium, and clerestory. However, since the arcade arches are exceptionally high, they minimize the architectural impact of the triforium and clerestory. The triforium is composed of large rounded arches, enclosing two smaller ones, with cushion capitals. Above this, the clerestory is composed of single round-headed (i.e., Norman) windows.

The massive plain circular piers alternate with compound-design piers. Shafts attached to the piers run from the floor to the ceiling then, at the clerestory level, flare inward to connect with and support the vault ribs. The piers

Nave looking east

are notable for their elaborate incised decorations (lozenges, zigzags, and chevrons). These features contrast with the earlier aisle walls. The arches are also decorated with spirals and chevron molding.

Note the small floor-mounted piers attached to the nave walls. Across the top of these, a series of stone half-rounds serve to interlink the piers. A carved string course that runs the length of these carvings helps tie this design together. These same decorations are found in the chapter house. Curiously, this same design was used in some old Muslim architecture.

Font Entering the cathedral one finds the impressive 1663 font set near the entry to the nave. The round font basin is made from white marble. Soaring above it is a heavily carved dark wooden canopy, resembling a tall Gothic spire. This wooden cover was the work of a Durham architect. Note also the large dark wood 17th-century organ case nearby, which originally sat atop the choir screen.

Ceiling The stone vaulting over the nave, finished in 1133, is of the simple four-part variety, while the ribs are decorated with yet more Norman carvings. The vault is supported by flying buttresses embedded in the aisle roofs.

Font with canopy

Windows The west end of the nave is dominated by a window in the exuberant Decorated style. The original mid-14th-century stained-glass window, depicting the Tree of Jesse story, was destroyed during the Reformation. It was restored in the late-19th century, reproducing the old design. Note the modern, brightly colored window "Daily Bread," near the north door.

➢ *Turn right into the Galilee Chapel [Floor Plan #3].*

GALILEE CHAPEL–LADY CHAPEL

The Galilee Chapel, which blocks the great west portal into the cathedral, was built around 1180 and is rather plain. The Lady Chapel was also placed here only because the sloping ground at the east end was unsuitable. There is also a legend that St Cuthbert was a misogynist who wanted to keep women from going inside the cathedral. Even today, one can see a black line on the floor inside the cathedral beyond which women could not pass.

Inside the chapel, on the north side, is the tomb of the famous early medieval scholar, the Venerable Bede, the father of English history. His bones were once covered with a splendid shrine, but destroyed by Henry VIII. His monument now consists of a plain marble slab with an inscription in Latin. Some walls of the chapel are decorated with a combination of medieval paintings, glass, and a modern window dedicated to Bede.

➢ *Proceed to the crossing [Floor Plan # 4].*

CROSSING CEILING

The ceiling of the central lantern tower above the crossing is remarkable for the gallery which runs around it. Even more dramatic is the four-pointed star design of the ceiling vault, which stands 155 feet (47m) above the floor.

➢ *Turn right into the south transept [Floor Plan #5].*

SOUTH TRANSEPT

This area has several interesting features, including:

Te Deum Window The large, six-panel window was erected about 1450. Some of the glass is ancient, but the greater part was installed only in the late-19th century.

St Gregory and DLI Chapels The modest St Gregory chapel and its modern window are dedicated to him. The DLI (Durham Light Infantry) chapel is loaded with colorful regimental banners.

Castelli's Clock Inside this transept is a colorful and complex old clock. It was installed during Prior Castelli's tenure (1494–1519), renovated between 1620 and 1638, and reconstructed again in 1938. It is the cathedral's only wooden object known to have survived the Civil War. As the story goes, its salvation was due to its being embellished with a thistle, the symbol of Scotland, and was therefore spared being used as firewood by the Scottish prisoners held here. The clock originally had only one hand and has an unusual face with 48 (instead of the usual 60) markings.

Next to it is the entrance to the central tower, a climb of 325 steps!

➢ *Pass through the choir screen portal into the choir area [Floor Plan #6].*

Castelli's clock

CHOIR AREA

This is the earliest part of the building—a blend of Norman and Early Gothic style architecture. The choir ceiling was vaulted in 1289, the ribs of which are decorated with dog-tooth moldings.

Choir Screen and Pulpit The original carved oak choir screen was destroyed in the mid-19th century. The present late-19th-century screen of marble and alabaster was designed and installed by George Scott. Although handsome, the screen's modest size and restrained design—three open Gothic arches with a carved gable in the upper center—fail to dominate the opening to the choir. Next to the choir screen is a particularly handsome pulpit, carved from stone matching that of the choir screen.

Choir Stalls This area was completed by the end of the 11th century. However, the elaborate carved woodwork on the choir stalls dates only from 1665, during the cathedral's restoration after the Civil War. As noted, the original stalls were used for firewood by the Scottish prisoners kept here by Cromwell's army. The tall Gothic canopies above and behind the stalls were perhaps inspired by the medieval stone screen behind the high altar. The misericord seats in the back row are full of carvings featuring lions, mermaids, monsters, apes, peacocks, and dolphins. The choir floor is paved with inlaid stone in an elaborate geometric design, somewhat similar to paving in front of the high altar at Westminster Abbey.

Organ The 17th-century organ was replaced in the late-19th century with the present organ. The earlier one had been destroyed by the Scottish prisoners. The organ is in two parts: one on each side of and above the choir stalls. Its pipes are beautifully painted with images of angels.

Organ pipe detail

Bishop Hatfield's Tomb–Throne East of the stalls stands the bishop's throne and tomb. This complex and highly decorated 14th-century construction is possibly the most extravagant combination of throne and tomb of a bishop in England. This bishop's throne is the tallest in England.

Bishop Hatfield throne–tomb

➢ *Continue into the high altar area [Floor Plan #7].*

HIGH ALTAR AREA

George Scott also designed this high altar, which replaced the 17th-century version. One of the treasures of the cathedral is the soaring, spiky stone screen—aka the Neville Screen—behind the high altar. It is elaborately carved in Gothic style and made of stone from Caen, France. Donated by Lord Neville, it was constructed in London around 1372 and shipped to Durham, where it was assembled. It was originally brightly painted, and alabaster statues of angels and saints would have filled each of its 107 niches. All these statues were destroyed during the Reformation. On either side of the altar and part of the screen are the stone seats for clergy.

High altar screen

➢ *Proceed into the south choir aisle and turn left [Floor Plan #8].*

SOUTH CHOIR AISLE

The south choir aisle has two notable modern windows: the "Millennium" window (1995) with its four-by-four brightly colored panes with scenes from St Cuthbert's life and the cathedral's history; and the "Transfiguration" window by Thomas Denny (2010), done with red and yellow glass. The monument of another bishop, Lightfoot, stands opposite.

One of the windows above this aisle has a small panel depicting a dyspeptic but nonetheless charming eagle. It is apparently a fragment left from a larger 15th-century window, which was broken.

➢ *Take the steps on the left up to the Shrine of St Cuthbert [Floor Plan #9].*

SHRINE OF ST CUTHBERT

Situated on a platform between the Neville Screen and the Chapel of the Nine Altars is all that remains of the famous shrine of St Cuthbert. Countless pilgrims came to make their offerings and seek his protection here in the Middle Ages. The depressions in the floor are said to have been worn by their feet. The vestments and other relics taken from his grave are kept in the library.

➢ *Continue into the Chapel of the Nine Altars [Floor Plan #10].*

CHAPEL OF THE NINE ALTARS

The Chapel of the Nine Altars is the major feature of the east end. Due to the sloping ground at the east end, this mid-13th-century construction resulted in a floor 6 feet (2m) lower than the cathedral floor. Extending across the entire east end of the building, this area is in effect a great hall where pilgrims would wait before entering St Cuthbert's shrine. It took 40 years to build this chapel, and the style developed as the work progressed. There are several special attractions here.

Joseph Window The six-panel stained-glass Joseph window on the north wall is one of the highlights of this chapel and is, indeed, one of the finest in England. The beautiful tracery design at the top is dominated by ten circles of varying sizes.

Rose Window The 18th-century copy of the 15th-century rose window is the other significant window. The design is based on the number 12. That is, there is a 12-element inner design showing the apostles surrounding Jesus in the oculus, while there are 24 such forms in the outer ring.

Other attractions include the nine lancet windows, each of which originally had its own separate altar. In addition, note the beautiful arcading whose deeply cut moldings are supported by slender shafts of white marble alternating with darker Purbeck. The nine original altars were dedicated to a series of saints.

➢ *Proceed into the north choir aisle and enter the north transept [Floor Plan #11].*

NORTH TRANSEPT

On the east wall of the north transept, the large window of the Four Doctors is in the Decorated style. As the name indicates, the panels depict four saints: Augustine, Ambrose, Gregory, and Jerome. It was restored several times, most recently in 1875.

➢ *Return to the nave and enter the cloister [Floor Plan # 12].*

CLOISTER

The late 14th-century cloister is located on the south side of the cathedral. Of interest is the oak ceiling, which is paneled and decorated with coats of arms. It was begun at the same time as the cathedral, but contains much work from the 15th century and later.

Cloister ceiling

Facing the cloister, the exterior of the Monk's Door has fine carvings of floral and other designs all over the arches and piers; the zigzag and double chevron designs are the most common. The intricate strapping on the door is a fine example of Norman ironwork.

The Prior's Door is the other old doorway, which also opens onto the cloister but further east. The large rounded arch is covered with Norman carvings, with each layer of arch molding supported by a number of side piers.

➢ *Turn into the chapter house [Floor Plan #13].*

CHAPTER HOUSE

The chapter house was built between 1133 and 1140. Then, in the 18th century, the "renovator" James Wyatt partially demolished it. This is yet another example of the destructive renovations carried out in later centuries. It has been recently restored. It is an architecturally interesting chamber, with an apsidal termination at the east end, an arcade of interlaced arches running around the wall, and rounded windows.

➢ *Enter the Open Treasure Gallery area [Floor Plan #14].*

OPEN TREASURE GALLERY AREA

Next to the Monk's Door, just inside the cloister, is the door with steps leading up to a separate L-shaped building complex. The Open Treasure Gallery is on the main floor that runs north and south. Directly above it is the former 14th-century monks' dormitory, a space so large that it was subdivided to form several residences after the Dissolution of the Monasteries in the 16th century. At the south end of this gallery, the building turns to the east, housing both the monastic great kitchen and the library.

Open Treasure Gallery This 194-foot (59m) long, beamed-roof complex occupies the whole of the western side of the cloister. It houses some of the most significant surviving Anglo-Saxon artifacts in the UK, including a number of Roman altars and tablets, as well as Saxon crosses and carved stones remarkable for their beautiful scroll-work. See also the famous Ruthwell cross, a stone from Hadrian's Roman wall, the monastic dining-table, the remarkable treasure-chest, plus the remains of St Cuthbert's coffin, which include his robes, and other relics taken from his tomb.

Great Kitchen The former monastery's kitchen is a remarkable octagonal space with a steeply vaulted ceiling. It is a separate structure accessed via the east facing area of the Open Treasure Gallery. It is surely worth a visit. Further to the east is the library.

Library Durham has many interesting manuscripts, including a copy of the early-8th-century Lindisfarne Gospels, taken by the monks when they fled in 875 CE and kept at the cathedral until seized at the Dissolution. Another treasure is a 7th-century manuscript, which once belonged to the Venerable Bede. The collection also includes three copies of the Magna Carta. Note that these are not among the four remaining "real" copies of the Magna Carta made at the time for distribution around the country. Lincoln Castle displays one of these, Salisbury another, and the British Library has the other two.

➢ *Exit into north door [Floor Plan # 1].*

PROFILES OF THE 13 CHURCHES
SOUTHWEST

St Andrew chapel, Gloucester

GLOUCESTER CATHEDRAL

Three-quarter view, east end

Personal Impressions

Gloucester Cathedral is set in the ancient port town of that name on the Severn River in the west of England. Many important early voyages to the New World began here, led by the likes of Walter Raleigh and Francis Drake. The town is a mix of modern-industrial and ancient buildings, as is the port itself. A sizable open space around the cathedral helps visitors' view in the midst of the surrounding neighborhood with its narrow streets.

Even from a distance, the feature that most catches one's eye is the central tower, decorated with open-work pinnacles. This design was the most graceful among all the cathedrals we visited, all lace-like elegance and lightness. One can see the sky through the open work.

Inside the cathedral excited us in particular because it is like a history lesson in medieval architecture. It is a study in Norman, Early Gothic, Decorated, and Perpendicular styles in an eclectic mix, which shifts from one style to another at every turn. And, although we don't always resonate with the modern additions to a medieval building, the recently installed windows in the south ambulatory and the Lady Chapel by the glass artist Thomas Denny are luminous and lovely.

The medieval stained-glass east window, installed in the 1350's, is one of the largest in Europe. Two other do-not-miss features are the large and special Lady Chapel, and the elaborately vaulted cloister. We agree with those who consider this cloister to be England's most beautiful.

History

From 681 CE an abbey occupied this site. To enhance its importance, in 1072 William the Conquerer appointed an entrepreneurial abbot from Mont St Michel in Normandy. This monk built up the wealth of the monastery to the point where in 1089 he was able to start constructing the present building. In 1327, Edward II, who was murdered nearby in Berkeley Castle, was buried here. His tomb attracted pilgrims and provided new wealth which stimulated further construction.

Henry VIII closed Gloucester Abbey in 1540 as part of his Dissolution. The abbey buildings became Gloucester Cathedral in 1541, now led by a bishop. Although Gloucester escaped the Civil War with little damage, the ideological and doctrinal struggles of the 16th and 17th centuries had an impact. The Lady Chapel was damaged by religious zealots, and the ultra-Protestant bishop was burned at the stake here in 1555 on the orders of the Catholic Queen Mary. Later, the ever-busy Victorians carried out many, not always positive, renovations. The cathedral was extensively restored during the last quarter of the 19th century.

Building

The masons experimented with designs based on the French style. Thus, the south transept became the earliest surviving example of English Perpendicular architecture. Next, the choir and high altar areas were redone using similar designs, which became the standard English style of architecture for centuries.

Gloucester Cathedral is of moderate size compared with the giants like Winchester and York. A surprising feature is that the 86 feet (26m) high choir ceiling is higher than the nave ceiling, which is only 69 feet (21m) high. The cathedral is unusual in other ways: it has only one tower, a rounded apse with an ambulatory, and only a single transept. Another odd feature is that the chapter house is in a separate building.

Exterior

WEST FRONT

The sparsely decorated west front is unremarkable. The entire west front is dominated by the large central window in the Perpendicular style. On each side are two more windows: the larger one on the right and the smaller on the left. Under the central window, there is a smallish single door with another (even smaller) door on the left side. At the top are two decorated pinnacles at each corner, connected by a screen of small arches.

SOUTH PORCH

This Perpendicular-style porch at the west end of the south wall is quite a display. It is the entrance to the cathedral and is heavily decorated with large statues on two levels, plus a Gothic frieze across the top. The figures depict saints including Peter and Paul.

TOWER AND BELLS

As noted, the 225 feet (69m) high central tower is one of England's most beautiful. This mid-15th-century tower is in the Perpendicular style and is covered with surface decoration, including a battlemented parapet with four tall, open-work pinnacles at the corners. The bells are ancient and were saved when the monastery was dissolved by Henry VIII.

Interior

Enter via the south porch [Floor Plan #1] to the nave [Floor Plan #2].

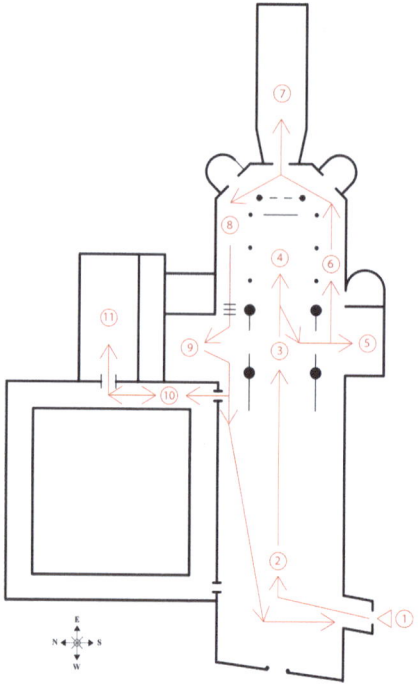

Floor Plan

1. South porch
2. Nave
3. Choir area
4. High altar area
5. South transept
6. South ambulatory
7. Lady Chapel
8. North ambulatory
9. North transept
10. Cloister
11. Chapter house

NAVE

The early-12th-century nave is a mix of stubby and plain Norman piers, Early Gothic vaults, and a Decorated south aisle. There is the usual three-level elevation, although the triforium is unglazed and is insignificant.

Piers and Arches The nave's 14 round Norman drum piers are huge at 6 feet (2m) across and 32 feet (10m) high. The low rounded arches are decorated with Norman zig-zag carvings. Note the series of grotesque heads between the nave arches.

Ceiling The simple Early Gothic ribbed vault connects to the piers by a cluster of shafts, which rise from corbels at the top of the triforium level. The vaulting over the nave stops abruptly at the juncture with the choir.

Nave

146   ENGLAND'S MARVELOUS GOTHIC CATHEDRALS AND CHURCHES

West Window The present glass was installed in the mid-19th century by William Wailes. The themes of the window are the birth of Jesus and the practice of Baptism. These are highly appropriate for the window's location, as baptismal fonts are usually placed near the west entrance to churches. Amusing bottom row panels include three water-related incidents from the Old Testament: Noah with his family, animals, and birds leaving the ark after the flood; Israelites after passing safely across the Red Sea; and a Syrian army commander washing in the Jordan to rid himself of leprosy.

West window

➤ *Proceed to the choir area [Floor Plan # 3].*

CHOIR AREA

This part of the cathedral occupies most of the crossing below the tower.

Choir Screen The medieval screen was replaced with the present, uninteresting, early-19th-century stone screen. It sits between the nave and the choir.

Organ The large handsome organ was installed in 1665 and has many highly decorated pipes. It sits on the top of the screen and is visible from both the nave and the choir areas.

Carved misericords

Choir Stalls and Floor The floor is elaborately tiled, and the choir stalls are backed with tall carved-wood canopies. The 46 medieval (and 12 modern) misericords are beautifully carved, with many curious scenes of hunting, such as St George slaying a giant.

Ceiling The complex rib-vaulted ceiling—which spans the crossing, choir, and high altar areas—is one of the finest in England.

➢ *Proceed to high altar area [Floor Plan #4].*

HIGH ALTAR AREA

Altar and Altar Screen Behind the high altar is the elaborately carved and painted altar screen with its three tall pinnacles and two side doorways. It was done by George Scott in 1873. As in several English Gothic churches, the otherwise simple altar is covered with a beautifully embroidered cloth.

Great East Window The east wall behind the high altar and screen consists almost entirely of this historic window, called the Crécy win-

Ceiling: crossing, choir, and high altar

dow, one of the greatest treasures of Gloucester Cathedral. Dating from the 1350s, this amazing window celebrates the famous 1346 battle, Edward III's first great victory over the French. The arms of Edward III, the Black Prince, and the famous lords who took part in the campaign against France at the battle of Crécy appear. The window emphasizes the sacred quality of kingship. It also depicts the Coronation of the Virgin with figures consisting of angels, apostles, saints, kings, and abbots.

The composition of the window is a grid with nine tiers of panel tracery covering the entire surface 72 feet (22m) high by 38 feet (12m) wide; the sides are bowed out. The present 1801 window is made up of medieval fragments gathered from elsewhere in the cathedral. The figures in the window are colored in red, white, and blue.

Look for a tiny charming scene in the lower right corner of the window which depicts what is said to be the first image of golf in the world. The game of golf may already have been known in the Netherlands by the late 13th century as "kolf," but it's a mystery how this image came to Gloucester soon after.

Whispering Gallery Behind and below the great east window is a long narrow passage built in the form of an octagon, called the Whispering Gallery. If one whispers at one side, every syllable may be distinctly heard on the other. A gallery at St Paul's, London, is said to have this same curious property.

➢ *Continue to the south transept [Floor Plan #5].*

SOUTH TRANSEPT

This transept is England's oldest surviving example of the Perpendicular style. It was converted from the original Norman style in the early-14th century. To modernize the interior of this transept the walls were covered with a stone veneer of Gothic tracery, and new windows were added beneath the Norman gables. Around the same time, a large internal flying buttress was added which cuts across the entire east wall at an angle. The architect clearly felt that strengthening that area was needed to support the tower. These changes provide an insight into what it took to transition from Norman to Gothic.

Great east window

South transept buttressing

The neo-Gothic Victorian-era St Andrews chapel at the east corner of the transept is covered with all manner of painting, striping, and lettering. Note that even the angled buttress shown above is covered with paintings on the chapel side, but not on the transept side. Other examples of internal buttressing can be seen as one proceeds through the cathedral.

➢ *Enter the south ambulatory [Floor Plan #6].*

SOUTH AMBULATORY

This rounded ambulatory has several interesting features.

Tomb of Robert Duke of Normandy Just outside the crypt is the tomb of Robert Duke of Normandy, who was King William's eldest son. He was notable for his performance during the crusades, but was an unsuccessful claimant to the English throne. Disagreement with his brother Henry I led to his captivity and death. His effigy was probably made not long after his death. It was hacked to pieces by Cromwell's soldiers, but the fragments were put back together. The chest on which it rests is 15th century.

Duke of Normandy tomb

New Stained-Glass Window As part of the 900th anniversary of the cathedral, the projecting chapel at the southeast corner of the ambulatory was refitted with a new blue-and-white stained-glass window by Thomas Denny. The center window depicts the New Testament story of Thomas in the presence of the risen Christ. The windows on either side are based on Psalm 148, praising God's creations.

➤ *Enter the Lady Chapel [Floor Plan #7].*

LADY CHAPEL

The area leading to the beautiful Lady Chapel is another meeting place of old and new work. The ambulatory is separated from the Lady Chapel by a screen. Entering the chapel, one first encounters a simple but elegant font—which dates from c.1130 and has fine figurative carvings.

New window by Denny

This Perpendicular-style chapel—built in 1225 and rebuilt in 1457—ranks with Ely's 14th-century Lady Chapel in size. The expansive main rear window is made up of medieval fragments. Each of the chapel's four bays has a lofty Perpendicular window, creating a wall of glass with paneled tracery. These side windows are from the Victorian Arts and Crafts era, depicting saints and biblical stories. Also see Denny's luminous 2013 window on the north wall. Small chantries open out from the Lady Chapel walls, each with fan vaults and singing lofts. Panels with niches cover the walls. The complex multi-ribbed vault is very fine, the bosses carved with beautiful foliage. Behind the altar at the east end is the dramatic carved stone screen with three large carved figures.

➤ *Continue to the north ambulatory [Floor Plan #8].*

NORTH AMBULATORY

The most important monument in the cathedral is no

Lady Chapel looking east

doubt the alabaster tomb of Edward II. He is said to have been murdered at the instigation of his queen at nearby Berkeley Castle. His reputation as an effete king is belied by his effigy here, which depicts him as a strong personality, with a full beard and the symbols of Plantagenet kingship. The face may have been copied from a death mask. Above is a canopy supported by arches, gables, a forest of pinnacles, and rich carvings. This part of the cathedral was "modernized" between 1331 and 1355. The updating was in part the result of the burial of Edward II, because Edward III wanted a more fitting burial place for his father.

The projecting chapel at the northeast corner of the ambulatory commemorates the Gloucester men who perished in various wars.

➤ *Enter the north transept [Floor Plan #9].*

NORTH TRANSEPT

This area demonstrates the further development of the Perpendicular style from the late-14th century. Note the interesting Reliquary of Decorated work, said by some to be a lavatory. The carved foliage is very beautiful as are the figures, although they are mutilated. Other highlights include:

Edward II tomb

Chapels The Chapel of St Anthony is on the south wall. In it, see a curious painting of St Anthony rescuing a female from the mouth of Hell. The transept has a 1615 monument, which bears the words: "Vayne, Vanytie. All is Vayne. Witnesse Solomon." On the east wall is the St Paul's Chapel, which retains its Norman form.

North Transept Screen Just below the north transept window, see the elegant mid-13th-century stone screen with three arches. The doorway into the treasury is in the center bay.

Clock The astronomical clock on the west wall is a Victorian installation. Its dramatic Art Nouveau design is black with gilt highlights. The clock features the 12 zodiac signs and 12 Roman numerals.

➢ *Enter the cloister [Floor Plan #10].*

CLOISTER

Gloucester Cathedral features the most spectacular and complete cloister in England. Dating from the mid-14th century, this cloister has the first fan vaulting in England, a revolution that would spread. Each of the four walkways around the cloister garden has its own fan vaulting.

In the north walkway, note especially the Victorian stained-glass windows in the lavatorium (the monk's communal washing place typically adjacent to

Cloister

the refectory). Made in 1868, these windows depict scenes from the Bible associated with water. On the south walkway are the monk's study niches with individual windows looking into the garden. The garden provides a good view of the central tower.

➤ *Proceed to the chapter house [Floor Plan #11].*

CHAPTER HOUSE

Constructed in the early 1080's, the chapter house is on the east side of the cloister. The monks would gather here daily for a reading of the Rule of St Benedict. Internal business was also transacted here. Today it is used for various cathedral events, including musical recitals.

➤ *Exit via the south porch.*

WELLS CATHEDRAL

Personal Impressions

The ride through beautiful Somerset County, and the combination of this lovely quiet town and bishop's palace compound, made Wells Cathedral special for us. Wells is considered to be the smallest city in England. As such, it is easy to get around and has kept its time-warp quality. Wells Cathedral is surrounded by many ancient buildings and is one of the first in England to be built entirely in Gothic style from the ground up.

With its broad west front and large central tower, the cathedral is the dominant feature of this petite city. By English Gothic church standards, Wells Cathedral is one of the smallest. The important thing about a medieval cathedral is not its statistics, but the sum of its features and the impression it makes.

Although some critics consider Wells to be one of the most beautiful of English Gothic churches, we found the west front rather block-like and too busy with decoration. But that is merely a matter of personal taste. We love the cathedral's setting, in the midst of its large grassy compound. The exterior feature we liked the most was the handsome central tower. By contrast, the two west

West front

front towers seemed truncated and blunt. We kept searching for non-existing pinnacles or crenellation.

On the inside, we were most fascinated by the modern-looking, dramatic scissors arches, the vaulted ceiling at the crossing, the entertaining old clock, and much of the old glass. This is altogether a wonderfully complex and delightful cathedral, set in its marvelous small town.

Wells has a large number of old buildings. In addition to the cathedral, we were enchanted by two nearby cathedral-related historical sites. One is the unique Vicars' Close, where the College of Vicars built accommodations for its chantry priests in 1348. It is connected to the cathedral via a covered bridge. To this day, choirmen are given accommodation in this small enclave, which preserves its picturesque medieval character.

Another delight was the 13th-century Bishop's Palace adjacent to the cathedral compound. An early bishop of Wells had a conflicted relationship with the locals, partly because of his imposition of taxes. To protect himself, he surrounded his palace with high walls, a moat, and a drawbridge. The highlight was its huge and remarkably well-maintained park-like garden. Within the garden is the source of the spring that is the basis of the adjacent stream and the name of Wells itself.

History

Wells Cathedral replaced an earlier church built on the same site in 705 CE. Work on the present cathedral commenced about 1175 at the eastern end with the building of the choir. Construction continued until 1490, but was complete enough to be dedicated in 1239.

Wells was never monastic, which may have helped it survive the Reformation's destructions better. However, its treasures were plundered by the infamous Duke of Somerset. During the Civil War, Cromwell's soldiers damaged the west front, tore lead from the roof to make bullets, broke the windows, smashed the organ and furnishings, and stabled their horses in the nave. Afterwards the cathedral fell into disrepair. The bishop left and some of the clerics were reduced to performing menial tasks.

By the middle of the 19th century, major restoration was made: The monuments were moved to the cloister, and the remaining medieval paint and whitewash removed in an operation known as "the great scrape." An extensive restoration program was done in recent decades, particularly of the west front. Current restoration efforts include the stained glass, particularly the large 14th-century Tree of Jesse window above the high altar.

Building

Access to the cathedral compound is via three ancient gateways: Brown's Gatehouse, the Penniless Porch Gate, and the Chain Gate. On the green is the 12th-century Old Deanery, largely rebuilt in the late-15th century. It is now used as offices for the diocese.

Some historians claim that Wells is the first truly Gothic cathedral in the world. It has piers with attached shafts rather than early style simple piers, and has a gallery of pointed arches. The nave, transept, and west front are fine examples of Early Gothic.

Exterior

WEST FRONT

This west front is a study in medieval theatricality. The lower and upper screen portions are rectangular, emphasizing width. This gives the west front a horizontal look, which is counteracted by the six attached vertical buttresses. This buttressing defines the cross-sectional divisions of nave, aisles, and towers.

The front rises in three distinct stages, each also clearly defined. The lowest level contains three plain portals, which are in stark contrast to the often imposing portals of French Gothic cathedrals. The outer doors are small, while the central door is ornamented by a central post, quatrefoil, and simple tympanum. The two levels above are ornamented with quatrefoils and niches, which originally held about 400 statues, 300 of which survived. Some have been restored or replaced, including the ruined figure of Christ in the gable. The top level consists of the two west towers and a central gable.

Altogether, the west front contains one of the largest galleries of medieval statues in the world. These major decorative features—done in the 1220's—include standing figures, seated figures, and half-size angels in high relief. Many of the figures are life-sized or larger. The figures and many of the architectural details had been painted in bright colors. The sculptures stretch horizontally across the entire west front and around the sides of the towers, which extend beyond the side walls. The vertical buttresses have tiers of niches which contain many of the largest figures. Other large figures, including that of Christ, occupy the gable. A single figure stands in one of two niches high on the northern tower.

NORTH PORCH

The north porch, located on the exterior nave wall, was originally the main entrance to the cathedral. This Early Gothic style porch is faced with a steeply arched door framed by rich moldings with eight shafts. The walls are lined with deep niches framed by narrow shafts with capitals like those of the portal.

TOWERS

West Front Towers The two west front towers—144 feet (44m) tall each—were erected in 1365, about 100 years after the central tower. The upper stages were built in the Perpendicular style. Although both towers are handsome, they were fitted with only a parapet, but not with pinnacles, which would have been a nice finishing touch.

Central Tower This 13th-century tower, which is 182 feet (55m) high, is Early Gothic up to the level of the roof. The section above that was added in the Decorated period and includes handsome pinnacles and other decoration. This upper addition risked disaster, however, as the foundations were unable to bear the additional weight. Skillful treatment was required, including installing bracing inside as well as adding flying buttresses.

Interior

➤ *Enter via the west front [Floor Plan #1] to the nave [Floor Plan #2].*

NAVE

Built between 1192 and 1239, the nave is Early Gothic, but Perpendicular tracery has been inserted in the windows.

Elevations The nave consist of three elevations: arcade at the bottom; the rudimentary triforium in the middle with a series of identical narrow openings; and the clerestory at the top which is the same height as the arcade. There are no vertical lines linking the three levels, as the shafts supporting the vault spring from carved corbels only at the triforium level. This helps emphasize the great length of the cathedral. The stonework of the pointed arcades and fluted piers is enriched by the complexity of moldings and carved capitals.

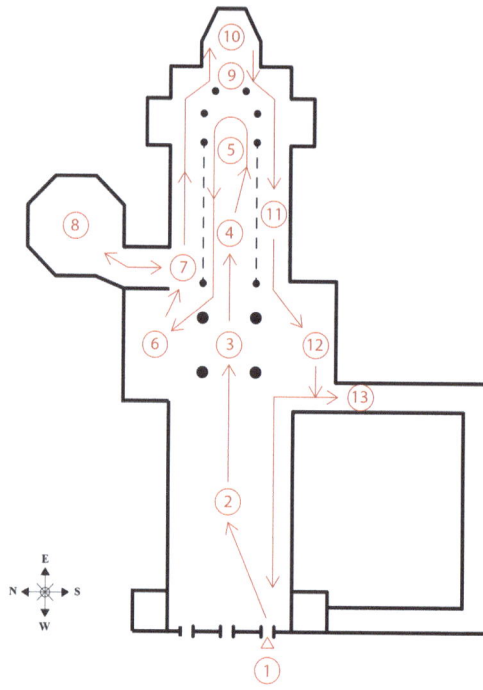

Floor Plan

1. West front
2. Nave
3. Crossing
4. Choir area
5. High altar
6. Main north transept
7. North choir aisle
8. Chapter house
9. East end
10. Lady Chapel
11. South choir aisle
12. Main south transept
13. Cloister

Arcade Arches and Piers The nave arcade arches are supported by massive compound piers. The surface of each pier has 24 slender shafts attached in eight groups of three. The capitals are decorated with fine carvings of stylized foliage, figures, faces, birds, animals, and monsters. And each capital is different. All elements combine to form an elegant structure.

Ceiling The steeply pitched four-part nave ceiling has charming stenciling which is said to represent a medieval Persian tree of life. The vaulting in the nave aisles is the same as the nave itself, but lacks stenciling.

Windows The large triple lancet windows at the west front were installed in 1664 and were repaired in 1813. The central pane, featuring Christ standing with a blue surround, was largely replaced in 1925–1931. These west windows are unexceptional modern work. The wall under the window consists of a rather odd series of piers on a plain slightly concave wall. There is also some 15th-century glass inside the tracery portions of the nave and transept windows, as well as 16th-century panes brought from a church in Rouen, France. They were installed in the 19th century.

Chapels and a Chantry Near the west front at the northwest corner of the nave is the Chapel of the Holy Cross, now used as a vestry. Across from it, at the southwest corner, is a former chapel, now allocated to the bell ringers. There are also two beautiful carved-stone chapels on each side of the nave altar.

Bishop Sugar chantry

The one on the left is Bishop Bubwith's chapel. On the right is Hugh Sugar's chantry whose fan-tracery of the roof, the niches, and the cornice of angels are worthy of notice, although the niches inside no longer have statues.

➢ *Continue to the crossing [Floor Plan #3].*

CROSSING

In the 14th century, the piers were sinking under the weight of the central tower. Strainer arches, commonly referred to as "scissor arches," were inserted to brace and strengthen the crossing. These famous and dramatic inverted arches flank the crossing on three sides: west, north, and south. The ceiling under the crossing tower is elegant, with four fan-shaped rib designs emanating from each corner. It is similar to the crossing ceiling at Winchester Cathedral.

➢ *Enter the choir area via the choir screen [Floor Plan #4].*

CHOIR AREA

The clerestory windows above the choir date from the early- to mid-14th century.

Choir Screen and Organ Constructed of carved stone, the choir screen is tall with five arches on each side of the entry portal. It has a three-level design, consisting mainly of empty niches of various

Scissor arches, crossing ceiling

WELLS CATHEDRAL

sizes. It is decorated with a modest amount of Gothic design over the doorway and at the top. Apparently it was even more handsome before the modern restoration. Atop the screen is the massive organ. Although a modern instrument, we find it graceful in its simplicity. It replaces the former late-14th-century organ which was destroyed by Cromwell's forces.

Organ-topped choir screen

Choir Stalls The choir stalls are still beautiful, although diminished by a mid-19th-century restorer, who destroyed most of the 16th-century woodwork. He then substituted it with stone canopies atop a wall separating the choir area from the north choir aisle. The finely embroidered seat backs under the stone canopies date from World War II. They help make the choir area even more stunning.

Embroidered seat backs

Misericord Carvings Apparently untouched by the renovators, the Decorated-style misericords date from the mid-14th century. The foci of the carvings is varied. It includes mythological subjects and stories, as well as a number of amusing human images. Amongst the many curious carvings are a mermaid, a griffin and various monsters, two goats butting, cats, peacock, chicken, fox and geese, lions, and rabbits.

Bishop's Throne and Pulpit The tall bishop's throne at the east end of the choir stalls is an extravaganza of Gothic designs executed in pure white stone. The back of the throne is lined with fine embroidered panels in rich colors. The less exuberant pulpit opposite the bishop's throne is made of finely decorated white stone.

Ceiling This ceiling covers both the choir and high altar areas. It was extended and decorated in about the mid-14th century. The vaulting has numerous ribs in a net-like, geometric form, which is very different from that of the nave. The ribs are dark, while the ceiling itself is a light color.

➢ *Continue to the high altar area [Floor Plan #5].*

HIGH ALTAR AREA

The high altar, with its opulent embroidered cover, has no altar screen. Instead, one sees directly into the east end of the cathedral. The highlight in this area is the mid-14th-century Tree of Jesse window which sits above the high altar. It shows the story of the birth, death, and resurrection of Jesus surrounded by his ancestors, all the way back to Jesse, father of King David. The combination of yellow and green glass, and the application of the bright yellow stain—rather than the usual reds and blues—give the window its popular name, the "Golden Window." It is flanked by two windows on

Tree of Jesse window, east window, and high altar

each side in the clerestory with large figures of saints, also dated 1340–1345. Although there are many Tree of Jesse windows in Gothic cathedrals, the Wells version is considered one of the finest. Legend has it that in the 17th century, in the process of destroying it, a soldier fell to his death. This may have discouraged others who had been tempted to do the same.

➢ *Proceed to the main north transept [Floor Plan #6].*

MAIN TRANSEPT

Wells has two transepts, the main one being at roughly the mid-point of the cathedral. This transept flanks the crossing on the north and south sides. The windows in both sides were installed in the early-20th century, replacing those destroyed earlier. The second transept is further east.

The main north transept has an astronomical clock from about 1325. It is the second-oldest surviving clock in England, after the Salisbury Cathedral clock. In addition to showing the time, it displays the motions of the sun and moon, the phases of the moon, and the time since the last new moon. The astronomical dial represents a pre-Copernican view of the universe, with the sun and moon revolving around a central fixed earth. At the striking of the clock, jousting knights appear above the clock face. Off to the right is another amusing feature of the clock: a seated figure who hits two bells with hammers, while hitting two more with his heels, on the quarter hour! The clock has its original medieval face but its mechanism was replaced in the 19th century. The original mechanism was moved to a museum in London, where it continues to operate.

There is a second face of the same clock on the outer wall of the transept, placed there about 70 years after the interior clock. Both clocks are driven by the same mechanism.

➢ *Enter the north choir aisle [Floor Plan #7], and turn into the chapter house [Floor Plan #8].*

CHAPTER HOUSE

Astronomical clock

The Decorated 14th-century interior has been judged to be architecturally the most beautiful in England. It is octagonal, with exotic fan vaulting, supported by a slender central pillar. The pillar is surrounded by shafts of Purbeck marble, rising to a single dark capital of stylized oak leaves and acorns. Branching out from the pillar are 32 prominent ribs, reminiscent of a palm tree.

The 51 stalls for clergy are richly carved, depicting numerous small heads of great variety, many of them smiling or laughing. The oldest surviving glass, dating from the late-13th century, is in the two windows on the west side of the staircase walking up. The chapter house windows are large with Decorated tracery. The tracery panes still contain ancient glass.

Fan-vaulted ceiling and windows

On the east wall of the steps leading to the chapter house, note the amusing corbel with the figure of a medieval man calmly subduing a dragon with his left hand while supporting a shaft with his right. This medieval stairway leads both to the chapter house and to the Vicars' Close via an enclosed bridge.

➢ *Enter the east end [Floor Plan #9].*

EAST END
The east end extends across the entire rear of the cathedral. At the center of the space, the vault is supported by a series of delicate Purbeck pillars: From each springs a forest of palm-tree ribs. All of the original glass from the 14th century is in the Lady Chapel and in the choir. This is one of the most important collections of medieval stained glass in England, despite damage by Cromwell's troops.

Chapels The many chapels located here include the following: the chapel of Corpus Christi in the northeast transept; St Stephen's chapel at the northeast corner; St John the Baptist's chapel at the southeast corner; and St Katherine's chapel in the southeast transept.

Bishop Bekynton Tomb Of greater interest is Bishop Bekynton's tomb, which is situated at the eastern entrance to the south choir aisle. Erected in the mid-15th century, this interesting tomb features two effigies: one of the bishop on top, and one below it of his imagined skeleton. The tomb is decorated with highly elaborate ribbed vaulting, which is painted and features pendants.

➢ *Enter the Lady Chapel [Floor Plan #10].*

LADY CHAPEL

This eight-sided Lady Chapel projects far out from the east end wall. It was completed by 1326. The features of interest are the vaulted ceiling and the east window.

Ceiling The vaulting here is unusual. The main ribs are intersected by additional non-supporting ribs, with a star-shaped pattern in the center, finished off with stenciling and a beautiful boss. It is one of the earliest such vaults in England.

East Window The east window, set above the tall altar screen, has five lancet panels, four of which date from 1325–1330 and include Old Testament figures, plus St Dunstan, a local saint who became Archbishop of Canterbury. This east window is flanked by two windows on each side. All four windows were restored to a semblance of their original appearance in the mid-19th century, using broken fragments of the original.

➢ *Go down south choir aisle [Floor Plan #11], and turn into the main south transept [Floor Plan #12].*

MAIN SOUTH TRANSEPT

Carvings The most interesting feature of this transept is the carving on the capitals, revealing not only the skill of medieval masons but also their wonderful sense of humor. Take the time to locate the series of both humorous and "story" carvings on various capitals, amongst which are a woman picking a thorn from her foot, and a man with a toothache. The most elaborate of them tells the story of a robber who tries to steal grapes from a vineyard and is caught.

Chapels On the east wall is the 14th-century chapel of St Calixtus, which contains finely carved white stone panels. Next to it is the chapel of St Martin, now a vestry. Buried here is the 15th-century Chancellor of Wells.

Font Set in the middle of the transept, the font is a legacy from the earlier Saxon church. Carved in the early-8th century, it predates the cathedral by more than 400 years, making it about 1,000 years old! The font is carved from plain white stone, but is topped with an extravagant gilt and red curved cover.

➤ *Turn into the cloister [Floor Plan #13].*

CLOISTER

The entrance to the cloister is via a doorway in the southwest corner of this transept. Since secular clergy—not monks—served this cathedral, the cloister was primarily ornamental, not the center of a monastic life. The most interesting feature of this cloister is the highly decorative rib-vaulted ceiling, which divides it into a number of curious shapes. The heavily traceried windows, although basically all grisaille glass, are handsome.

➤ *Exit via the west front.*

Carvings on capitals

Exeter Cathedral

West front

Personal Impressions

This city seems at first to consist entirely of old brick and dark-brown stone 19th-century buildings. Fortunately, the walk up to the cathedral area is graced with lovely buildings and tree-filled neighborhoods. The cathedral sits in its own grassy park-like space in an historic district, although much of that area is now quasi-commercial.

And what a charming cathedral this is! We liked it from the first moment. Surrounded by a large and gentle slope on its front and north sides, the cathedral is set off from the mostly modern town around it. Easily the most arresting feature of the exterior is the screen-design west front, filled with niches and many statues of saints, kings, and nobles. It is said that the Bible-related sculptures were put there mainly to teach illiterate people what Heaven looked like. Owing to the weather and the rather porous local sandstone, many of the sculptures, especially on the lower panels, are badly damaged. Originally heavily painted, now only tiny remnants of red, blue, or green hint at its former glory. Nonetheless, the sculptural display still shows what the west front was like.

On the inside, the cathedral's long, uninterrupted vaulted ceiling creates the illusion of a long church. The interior is loaded with many fine features, most of which are old—not Victorian copies—and beautifully executed. Note the colorful tombs, interesting bosses on the nave ceiling, the bishop's splendid chair, painted choir screen, and the rare minstrel's gallery.

There is an old Roman wall alongside a path that leads into the town at the rear of the cathedral. It's worth walking it to get a feeling for the ancient history of this site.

History

Exeter Cathedral dates from 1050. A Saxon minster already existed within the town, but held services often out of doors close to the site of the present cathedral building. In the early-12th century, William the Conqueror's nephew was appointed bishop. He began building a new cathedral in the Norman style. It was officially consecrated in 1133, but took many more years to complete. In about 1258, the building was rebuilt in the Decorated style, following the example of Salisbury, about 100 miles away. However, much of the Norman building was kept, including the two massive square side towers and part of the walls. The present building was finally completed by about 1400, except for the chapter house and chantry chapels. In general, the Gothic additions were grafted onto the original, thick-walled Norman church.

Like many English cathedrals, Exeter suffered during the Reformation even though it was secular, not monastic. The Civil War was also a tumultuous period for the cathedral. When the city was captured by Parliamentary forces in 1646, the chapter was disbanded and the cloister destroyed. The city council then decided to allow worship by both Presbyterians and Congregationalists. To accommodate both groups, a wall was built to divide the church in two, with the Presbyterians in the choir and the Congregationalists in the nave.

In 1942, the Germans bombed the cathedral, destroying the St James chapel, three bays of the aisle, and two flying buttresses. The bomb also destroyed the medieval wooden screen opposite the St James chapel, which is now restored.

Thanks to the prudent removal of Exeter's treasures, there was no damage to the ancient glass, the misericords, the bishop's throne, the ancient charters of kings Athelstan and Edward the Confessor, and other precious documents.

Building

A prominent feature of Exeter Cathedral is its stylistic unity, which it has in common with Salisbury and Wells cathedrals. Exeter is one of the English Gothic churches with a "screen front." Although large, the screen front here is more modest than the extravagant one at Lincoln Cathedral. The Norman towers at each end of the transept stand out noticeably from the side walls. As is the norm for English Gothic churches, the east end is squared off, rather than rounded in the French fashion—or it would be square if the Lady Chapel didn't project out so far from the eastern wall.

Special features of the interior include the degree to which the coloring has been restored to various architectural details, such as the roof bosses and corbels in the nave, as well as various arches and vault ribs. In addition, unlike nearly every other medieval cathedrals in England, Exeter has no shrine to a saint.

Exterior

WEST FRONT

Completed in 1375 the west front is jammed with every decorative trick in the designer's repertory. The screen portion of the front is divided into three tiers, one above the other. The lowest tier depicts angels; above them are statues of kings, knights, saints and apostles. Although eroded, the figures clearly show animated postures and individual personalities. The gable at the top features a tall modern sculpture of St Peter.

A dominant feature of the west front is the beautiful, heavily traceried, arched central window with a large rose window inset at the top. Another, smaller window is set at the top of the gable. The three west portals are small, which is the English tradition. The large central one is the only portal with carved molding.

TOWERS AND BELLS

The 12th-century Norman side towers at each end of the transept were originally separated from the cathedral. The towers are stolid and square, lacking in decoration except for the four plain pinnacles atop each. The north tower contains an 8,000 lbs (3,629 kilos) chiming bell, named Peter. The south tower encloses the second heaviest of the bells, which weighs 7,200 lbs (3,266 kilos). This tower holds one of the heaviest sets of 12 change-ringing bells in the world.

Interior

➢ *Enter via the west front [Floor Plan #1] to the nave [Floor Plan #2].*

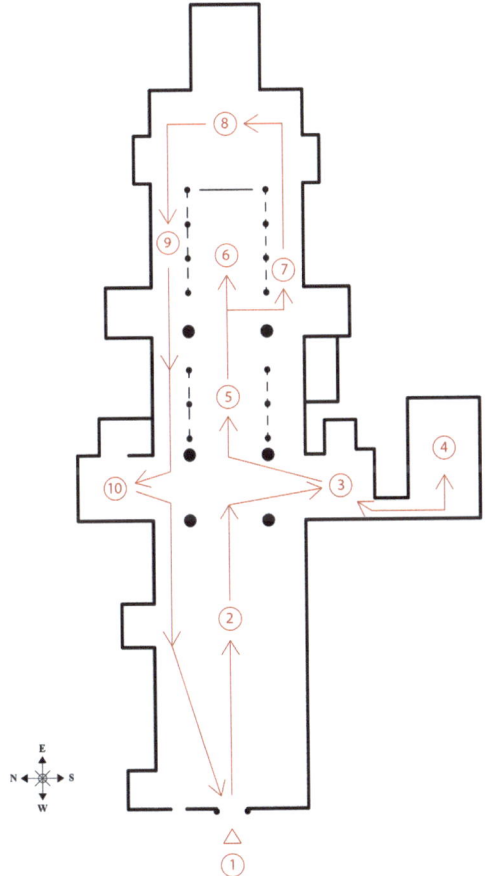

Floor Plan

1. West front
2. Nave
3. South transept
4. Chapter house
5. Choir area
6. High altar area
7. South choir aisle
8. East end
9. North choir aisle
10. North transept

NAVE

The nave was constructed almost entirely in the Norman style, then converted to the Decorated, enjoying many rich architectural and decorative details. The clustered Purbeck marble piers are composed of 16 slender shafts, which help support the ceiling. Each arch has many ornamental moldings.

Nave looking east

Chapel of Bishop Grandisson This chapel is on the right as one enters the cathedral. It is decorated with a carved figure of Jesus, his hand outstretched to bless. There are holes in the stone for suspending lamps.

Ceiling The most notable feature of Exeter Cathedral may be the enormously long vaulted ceiling. At 315 feet (96m), it is the longest continuous vault in Europe. The architects were able to do this because there is no central tower to interrupt the continuity. In contrast to its length, the ceiling is only 66 feet (20m) high—one of the lowest in England. The vaulted ceiling is a virtual forest of ribs: each side of the central ridge rib is connected to 11 ribs in each bay that sprung from a single corbel below the clerestory. Many beautifully carved bosses stud the ceiling, depicting foliage, animals, exotic figures, and heraldic shields. Look for the first ceiling boss at the west end of the nave, which depicts the murder of St Thomas Becket. Notice the interesting sculptured and colored corbels between the arches as well.

Wall corbels and ceiling boss

Font To the right of the entrance, the handsome font is made of carved white Sicilian marble. The different rounded and pointed top is composed of dark oak wood.

West Window The glass in this colorful window was installed in the mid-18th century. The window is in the usual pointed arch shape, but is distinctive due to the rounded rose design at the top. The center of the rose is occupied by a stylized five-pointed figure. It has nine tall glass panels below, divided into two rows. The upper row of the central panel is a depiction of St Peter holding the keys. The eight flanking panes show royalty and miscellaneous clerics. The bottom row is a series of coats of arms.

West window

Nave Windows The squat, unglazed nave triforium has four small arches for each bay. By contrast, the clerestory windows are large, and each aisle-level bay is filled with a single window. All these windows are in the Decorated style and have a variety of elaborate tracery patterns. They are arranged in pairs, each window corresponding to the one opposite.

Minstrel's Gallery

Minstrel's Gallery Unique among English cathedrals, the 14th-century Minstrel's Gallery is at the triforium level on the north side of the nave. The gallery has 14 painted angels, each playing a different medieval instrument. These include a type of zither, bagpipe, hautboy, harp, trumpet, organ, guitar, and cymbals. For hundreds of years, musicians played in this gallery on high festival days or for visits of royalty.

EXETER CATHEDRAL

Pulpit carving detail

Pulpit Also called the "Martyrs' Pulpit," this was designed by George Scott in the 1870s in memory of John Coleridge Patteson, who was ordained in Exeter Cathedral but devoted much of his life to the peoples of the Pacific Islands of Melanesia, becoming their first Bishop. He was murdered in the Solomon Islands in 1871, and the central pulpit panel depicts the islanders placing his body in a canoe to be returned to his ship. Other pulpit panels portray additional saints and martyrs. The astonishingly finely detailed carvings give the impression of wood although this is actually a stone pulpit supported by a series of piers.

➢ *Proceed to the south transept [Floor Plan #3].*

SOUTH TRANSEPT

Monuments This area is loaded with monuments, most notably the one to Hugh Courtenay who was the late 14th-century second Earl of Devon and his wife Countess Margaret. Also note the one to the Cornwall Light Infantry. This flag-bedecked chapel is decorated with the military flags carried at Waterloo and in the Indian Mutiny.

Organ Pipes Note the array of giant organ pipes along the west wall. These pipes produce the organ's lowest tones. The longest of them is 36 feet (11m) tall.

Ceiling and Balustrade The ribbed, wooden ceiling in this transept is a fine work of architectural art. Another noteworthy feature is the carved white-stone balustrade with flaring supports high on the wall.

➢ *Continue to the chapter house [Floor Plan #4].*

CHAPTER HOUSE
The fine wooden ceiling with carved and painted angels is surely one of the most beautiful in any Gothic church. Notice the 13th-century Early Gothic design of the arcade in the lower part. A number of large, sculptural figures fill the niches along both long walls.

➢ *Enter the choir area [Floor Plan #5].*

Ceiling detail

CHOIR AREA
Choir Screen This beautiful 14th-century choir screen is made from white stone and has three large arched doorways. Across the top is a line of 11 small decorated arches, which are uncommon. Inside each archway is a 17th-century painting of biblical scenes. The carved foliage in the spandrels between the arched doorways is especially fine.

Organ The large organ sits dramatically on top of the choir screen. Built in 1665, it is one of the oldest in England and has been renovated many times since. The contrast between the organ pipes and dark wood organ case is striking.

Choir Stalls, Canopy, and Misericords In the early-14th century, the choir area was redone in the Decorated style. Lining the walls above the stalls is a tall dark wood canopy, heavily carved. The back

Choir screen

Choir and organ looking west

EXETER CATHEDRAL

rows of the 19th-century choir stalls contain 49 misericords. The mid-13th century carvings on the stalls and misericords are the oldest in England and often whimsical. Particularly note the carving of an elephant. As the story goes, this was inspired by an elephant kept in the Tower of London by Henry III.

Bishop's Throne This magnificent throne sits at the east end of the choir stalls. Terms like extravagant don't begin to describe it. Crafted from oak between 1312 and 1316, the 59-foot (18m) high throne was removed from the cathedral for safekeeping during World War II. The throne is a magnificent piece of craftsmanship by any standards.

➢ *Continue into the high altar area [Floor Plan #5].*

HIGH ALTAR AREA

Unlike most other churches, there is no altar screen, only a low carved-stone wall and two rounded arch openings below the great east window.

High altar area

Great East Window This large window was damaged in World War II. Even so, the present window, composed of mainly 14th-century stained glass, is handsome. In addition to spreading across the entire width of the high altar area, the window takes up some two-thirds of the rear wall elevation with nine vertical glass panels. The top half is full of tracery and colorful panes.

Bishop Stapledon's Tomb Bishop Stapledon's tomb to the left of the altar is worthy of note. A handsome carved stone arch sits above his effigy, dressed in blue- and gray-colored clothing.

Stone Benches To the right of the altar, the stone benches for clergy should not be missed. They are topped with an elaborately carved canopy.

➢ *Enter the south choir aisle [Floor Plan #7].*

SOUTH CHOIR AISLE

St James Chapel and Carved Wooden Screen A beautifully carved wooden screen at this side entrance to the choir area and the medieval chapel were demolished by German bombs in 1942. Both were reconstructed after World War II in the original style, but with some 20th-century details.

Carved Ceiling Boss On the floor, near the St James chapel, is a full-sized reproduction of the central boss of the cathedral. It depicts a knight on horseback. The original boss decorates the ceiling at the center of the crossing. Visitors will be surprised at the size of the boss, and how colorful it is.

➢ *Proceed to the east end [Floor Plan #8].*

EAST END

The east end has several notable tomb-chapels and other features of interest. As one enters the east end, note the following from right to left.

Bishop Oldham Chapel This chapel is in the southeast corner. Bishop Oldham's emblem, an owl, is carved on every surface of the walls and ceiling. One rarely sees such a proliferation of owl images.

St Gabriel Chapel–Bishop Bronescombe Tomb On the right as one faces the Lady Chapel, the St Gabriel chapel has a ceiling painted a rich blue, studded with moons and stars, and crisscrossed with a network of ribs. Every junction is fitted with gilt bosses. The canopied tomb of Bronescombe contains a brightly colored effigy, heavily gilded and painted.

Lady Chapel Projecting far beyond the east wall, the Lady Chapel contains prominent features, such as East Window and Lady Dodderidge tomb.

Set above a carved stone canopy behind the altar, this large, handsome east window is seven panels high, with a rounded wheel design at the upper level. All of the glass is colored. Before the bombing in World War II, this window had darker glass. On the north wall is the effigy of the finely dressed Lady Dodderidge, recumbent, her hand resting on a skull.

Lady Dodderidge tomb

Bishop Stafford Tomb – St John the Evangelist Chapel This tomb–chapel is on the left as one faces the Lady Chapel. It is nearly identical to the St Gabriel chapel–Bishop Bronescombe tomb on the right. They flank the entrance to the Lady Chapel. This chapel is as highly painted and decorated as the other. Note particularly the striking ceiling.

➢ *Proceed to the north choir aisle [Floor Plan #9].*

NORTH CHOIR AISLE

Entering the north choir aisle, to the right is the chapel of St. George (aka, the Speke Chantry). The ceiling is most unusual, all three-dimensional roundels studded with stubby pendants. Note the ceiling bosses which show the Savior's head and the emblems of the Evangelists. The other memorable thing about this chapel is the ancient painting on the door depicting St. Apollonia (the patron saint of dentists!). She is carrying a tooth in a pair of long pincers.

➢ *Enter the north transept [Floor Plan #10].*

NORTH TRANSEPT

Astronomical Clock This marvelous clock dates from 1484. The fleur-de-lys hand indicates the time (and the position of the sun) on a 24-hour analog dial, consisting of two sets of I–XII Roman numerals. The silver ball and the inner dial represent the phases of the moon. The upper dial, added in 1760, shows the minutes. The Latin phrase on the clock is translated as "They perish and are reckoned to our account," referring to the hours that we spend, wisely or not. The original mechanism was modified, repaired, and finally replaced in the early-20th century.

Cat Door The door below the clock has a small round opening at the bottom. This opening was cut in the early-17th century to allow the bishop's cat to keep out the vermin attracted to the animal fat used to lubricate the mechanism. As legend has it, the cat was contracted for at a penny a week.

Also note the Chapel of the Holy Cross (aka the Sylke Chantry) and the St Paul's chapel which is on the east wall of this transept and is now used as the vestry.

➢ *Exit via the west front.*

Salisbury Cathedral

West front

Personal Impressions

The large grassy compound surrounding the cathedral is peaceful and scenic. Its venerable old fortification walls were erected in the time of Edward III. Outside these walls, quiet lanes are lined with a lovely mix of medieval and elegant Georgian dwellings.

Since we had seen paintings of the cathedral by J.M.W. Turner and John Constable, we had felt quite familiar with this iconic building. Not quite so. The real thing was far better. That soaring, beautiful spire is easily the greatest in England.

The cathedral has many other special features, including what is probably the most elegant chapter house in England. That said, this is one of the "plainest" of English Gothic churches on the inside. However, the interior conveys a feeling of lightness and elegance. It is like touring a museum and encountering many fine discrete elements when proceeding from room to room. Surprisingly, the most emotionally captivating piece was the contemporary baptismal font.

All who have experienced this cathedral express admiration, even affection for it. We are no exception.

A short walk into this charming medieval town offers other historic attractions. For us, the old St Thomas Church was especially interesting. Note the marvelous so-called 'Doom Painting' at the end of the nave above the arched entrance. It's worth a visit to see this painting and the church's coffered wood ceiling.

History

The shrine of 11th-century Bishop Osmund was built to be a spectacular centerpiece in the Trinity Chapel as part of the cathedral's competitive efforts to attract pilgrims. Nonetheless, Salisbury never became a major place of pilgrimage like Canterbury and Winchester. Still it is packed with monuments and shrines to famous people and military organizations from the past.

During the Reformation, St Osmund's shrine was destroyed, the chantries abolished, and the relics of the saints and stone altars were replaced with wooden tables. Bad as that was, Salisbury and other purely secular cathedrals suffered less damage than, say, Canterbury and Durham, which originated as monasteries.

During the Civil War, the bishop was pushed aside, his palace mostly demolished, the clergy expelled, their houses and property seized, and the glazing in the upper windows was destroyed and never replaced. In addition, a great deal of lead was stolen from the roofs. The damaged cloister was used for a time to keep Dutch prisoners.

Renovations and conservation began in the 17th century and have continued to the present time. But disaster struck in the 18th century when the "destructive" James Wyatt went to work. After closing the cathedral from 1789–1792, he demolished what remained of the free-standing bell tower and two porches. He also completely changed the interior: by removing the two medieval chapels at the east end and all remaining medieval glass; by whitewashing the medieval wall murals and vaulting decorations; by moving monuments; and by building a new choir screen.

In the 19th century, George Scott reversed much of this earlier damage. In 1960, however, the clergy removed Scott's choir and high altar screens to provide an unobstructed view from the entrance to the east end.

The Building

Although we haven't tried to compare English cathedrals, Salisbury must have more special characteristics than any other. For example, it has: the tallest spire in Britain (404 feet, 123m); the best preserved of the four surviving original copies of the 1215 Magna Carta; the oldest working clock in Europe (1386); the largest cathedral cloister and cathedral compound in Britain; and the largest and earliest complete set of choir stalls in Britain. Not least, Salisbury Cathedral shares with Wells the distinction of being the first English cathedral during the Middle Ages built from scratch in the Gothic style.

This Early Gothic style cathedral was erected in record time—only 100 years. Construction began in 1220, with the foundations of the Lady Chapel. It was finished by 1320 with the erection of the tower and spire. Since construction was carried out more or less nonstop, the building has an unusual unity of design. The short building time contrasts with most other English Gothic churches, which were renovations of existing Norman churches.

A 15th-century bishop reconstructed the eastern end, including the Trinity Chapel. He also installed the stone vault above the crossing. The other notable changes came with the building of new chapels.

Important features include the cathedral's great length of 473 feet (144m), as well as a vault height of only 84 feet (26m). This followed the general pattern in England, where the emphasis was on the horizontal dimension: long churches with low ceilings. In addition, the foundations are only four feet deep, due to the high water table here near the River Avon. The site has flooded many times.

Given its unstable foundations, Salisbury has buttresses everywhere one looks, inside and out. On the exterior south wall and central tower, there are heavy buttresses which connect to the clerestory level; even the relatively low walls of the cloister have thick attached buttresses. Likewise, the interior has both visible and hidden buttresses which help support the crossing under the tower. Most noticeable are the large strainer arches in the nave, which divide the choir aisles from the transept. Note the dramatic, makeshift-looking bundles of shafts supporting the base of the central tower. There are also partially hidden buttresses behind the triforium and clerestory openings throughout the cathedral.

Exterior

WEST FRONT

Some architectural critics assert that Salisbury's west front is little more than a jumble of architectural motifs, at least as compared with Wells Cathedral, which has been called "the prototype of English screen-façades." We feel this to be an overly harsh judgment about what is primarily a matter of individual taste.

The front is punctured with 130 shallow niches of varying sizes, 73 of which contain a statue. All but eight of the remaining statues are Victorian. The line of niches extends around both sides. There are five levels of niches. The upper level depicts angels and archangels, Old Testament patriarchs, apostles and evangelists, martyrs, doctors, and philosophers. Lower-level statuary represents royalty, priests, and worthy people connected with the cathedral. While the majority of the statues are 19th century, seven are from the 14th century and several have been installed within the last decade.

The façade has two turrets—not towers—one at each corner, and there is a large, three-lancet window in the center of the west front. The turrets are topped with pinnacles, while the central section is topped by a gable with four lancet windows. Surmounting all this is a statue of Christ.

The principal entry to the cathedral is flanked by two smaller doors. On the tympanum above the main door notice the handsome and unusual carvings depicting the Virgin and Child, flanked by angels.

TOWER AND SPIRE

The single tower–spire epitomizes the cathedral's image. The tower alone is 225 feet (69m) high, and with its spire it is 404 feet (123m) high. The spire is embellished with three carved horizontal bands. The original design called for a square crossing tower of modest height. But in the early part of the 14th century, two stories were added, and then the pointed spire was added. Note how it transitions from square to octagon shape. It is a work of art in its own right.

Interior

➢ *Enter via the west front [Floor Plan #1] to the nave [Floor Plan #2].*

NAVE

The openness of the nave gives the impression that it is a huge space. One cannot help but feel one's smallness in contrast. What greets the visitors first is the contemporary font. The cruciform-shaped "Living Water" font by British sculptor William Pye is a marvel, installed here in 2008 to commemorate the 750th anniversary of the cathedral. It sits in the middle of the nave about halfway down. The water reflects various features of the interior depending on where one stands. It may be the most beautiful font we have seen. Despite its modern look, it fits right into the Gothic architecture.

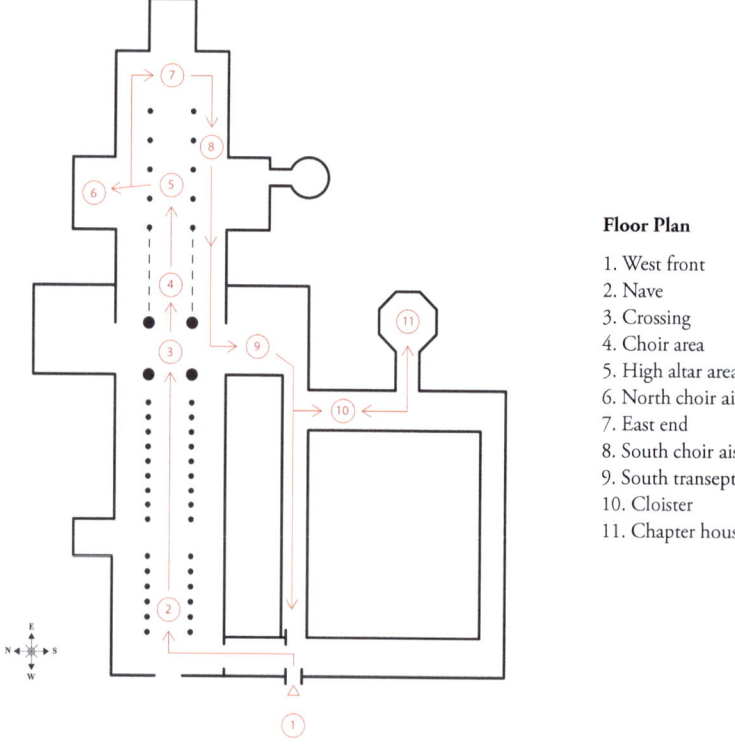

Floor Plan

1. West front
2. Nave
3. Crossing
4. Choir area
5. High altar area
6. North choir aisle
7. East end
8. South choir aisle
9. South transept
10. Cloister
11. Chapter house

The nave has the usual three-level elevation, although the arches take up about half the total nave height, relegating the triforium to being a bit player. The ceiling vaults here are rather plain as are the arcades. However, the piers are a handsome assembly of Purbeck marble shafts. Oddly for an entirely post-Norman church, there are no floor-to-ceiling shafts to direct one's eyes upward to the old-style four-part ribbed vaults. Instead, the ribs spring from corbels situated at the base of the clerestory level.

Nave looking west

West Window The west window consists of fragments of old glass saved from earlier destruction. With some effort, it may be possible to discern the figure of Christ, the Virgin, and the Adoration of the Magi. Throughout the cathedral, essentially all the old glass is gone, thanks to the Puritans and to the notorious renovator Wyatt. However, due to the large amount of clear glass and the light-colored stone, the interior illumination is excellent.

Clock The 14th-century clock sits on the north aisle wall across from the entrance. Known to be the world's oldest working mechanical clock, it has no face because such clocks rang out the hours on a bell. The clock was originally located in the free-standing bell tower demolished in the late-18th century. It was moved to the tower where it functioned until 1884, then placed in storage and forgotten, but discovered in 1929 in an attic. The mechanism was repaired and restored to working order in 1956. Historians calculate that is has ticked more than 4.4 billion times since it was built.

Tombs Most of the memorials are located between the piers which divide the nave and side aisles. This contributes to the feeling of spaciousness in the nave. The two most interesting memorials are across the nave aisle from each other. The tomb of Lord John Cheney is on the north side. Sir John was one of Henry Tudor's bodyguards at the Battle of Bosworth, where he recovered Henry's standard after its bearer was killed. Sir John was then wounded by

Richard III before Richard himself was killed and Henry Tudor proclaimed king. The tomb is life-sized and carved from white marble.

On the south side is the tomb of William Longspe. This knight was the half-brother of King John and the illegitimate son of Henry II. He was the first to be buried in the cathedral. His life-sized, helmeted effigy is presented dramatically with him holding a large shield in his left hand. The effigy rests on a carved and painted chest.

➢ *Continue to the crossing [Floor Plan #3].*

CROSSING

Originally, the tower–spire was supported only by four interior piers here at the crossing. After the spire's 6,400 tons of weight was added, the piers bent nine inches from the vertical. This buckling can be seen today. To balance it, 112 wood and stone buttresses were added. The next step was to build the strainer arches to each side of the central crossing. Reinforcing beams above the crossing, designed by Christopher Wren in 1668, diminished threats of collapse. These beams are hidden by a false ceiling, installed below the lantern stage of the tower. The spire soared so high that iron bands were attached to stabilize it in the wind. Despite this, the spire has tilted 27½" to the southeast.

Ceilings: crossing, choir, and high altar

Had it not been for the addition of buttresses, strainer arches, and other supports, Salisbury would have suffered the fate of other churches whose spires had fallen down. Continuing worries about the stability of the structure led in 1950 to the rebuilding of the top of the spire and to an ongoing conservation program.

Note the elegant square ribbed ceiling under the tower, with the star-shaped rib design at the center.

In the crossing, at the entrance to the choir, is a handsome pulpit made of beautifully carved white marble. It is supported by a series of small piers and is topped with a canopy.

➢ *Proceed to the choir area [Floor Plan # 4].*

CHOIR AREA

There is no choir screen, the Victorian screen having been removed. There is old Perpendicular work in the choir, and some later work by Christopher Wren. All else is new.

Organ The current organ was built in 1877. The pipes are mounted on the side walls above the choir stalls. An earlier organ presented by George III was installed on top of the stone choir screen at the time. It was later taken out and moved to St Thomas Church in the town.

Choir Stalls The 106 stalls date from 1236, although some are new. They are decorated with many fine carvings.

Bishop's Throne At the east end of the choir area is this grandiose confection of dark wood, with a tall carved canopy. A few cathedrals have even more elaborate ones!

Ceiling The ceiling above the choir and the high altar area is the same. Although it has simple early looking four-part rib vaults, the open spaces between the ribs are handsomely painted with multiple roundels in each of the four parts. Each roundel painting depicts Jesus or other biblical characters.

➢ *Continue to the high altar area [Floor Plan #5].*

HIGH ALTAR AREA

There is no screen or structure between the high altar and the east end of the cathedral. However, the eastern wall, dominated by three tall arches and topped with three lancet windows, ends this area nicely. The notable feature here is the 16th-century chapel of Bishop Audley to the left side of the altar. It is a small but fine chapel, up a few steps, with an elaborate fan-vaulted, painted ceiling.

Bishop Audley chapel

➢ *Proceed to the north choir aisle [Floor Plan #6].*

MORNING CHAPEL

Projecting from the north aisle, this large chapel is lined with tall lancet windows. It has two altars: one with a handsome altar screen decorated with red and green panels; another on the north wall with a reliquary and decorated arches. Separating this chapel from the north choir aisle are the remnants of the former 14th-century choir screen. The destructive Wyatt moved the screen here from the front of the choir in the 18th century.

➢ *Proceed to the east end [Floor Plan #7].*

EAST END AREA

The east end consists primarily of the Trinity Chapel, the Lady Chapel, and the tomb of the Earl of Hertford and wife.

Trinity Chapel While this chapel is little more than an ante-room to the large Lady Chapel, it has beautifully clustered pillars and fine vaulting.

Lady Chapel This lovely chapel, which is the oldest part of the cathedral, extends beyond the eastern wall. The modern, brilliant blue east window is called the "Prisoners of Conscience Window," made by a French artist Gabriel Loire. Installed in 1980, this five-arched window replaced earlier windows. Although dedicated to human rights, the depictions focus mainly on biblical themes.

"Prisoners of Conscience Window" by Loire

Earl of Hertford and Wife's Tomb At the southeast junction of the Trinity Chapel and south choir aisle is the tall, elaborate tomb of the unlucky 16th-century Earl of Hertford and his wife. He married the sister of Lady Jane Grey, incur-

Earl of Hertford and wife tomb

ring Elizabeth I's resentment. Imprisoned by the queen, it is believed that her time in the tower and separation from her husband caused her early death. Note that her effigy is somewhat elevated relative to his. This was due to her royal connections, which gave her a higher status, despite her family's disgrace.

➢ *Proceed down the south choir aisle [Floor Plan #8].*

VESTRY

Jutting out from the south choir aisle is the vestry. Of interest are the elegant, rounded strainer arches at the entrance across the doorway leading into the choir and high altar areas. The painted ceiling and three-level array of windows are noteworthy.

After exiting the vestry, just before the transept, note the handsome tomb of the 13th-century Bishop Bridport.

➢ *Continue to the south transept [Floor Plan #9].*

SOUTH TRANSEPT

The south transept at the crossing is very similar to the north transept, especially as regards the vaulting and the three-level window treatments on the façade of each. In addition, both have some old wooden screens. This transept has three chapels, the most notable is the St Michael chapel at the far end. It is dedicated to Britain's armed forces. Wooden screens between the piers separate the main space from the side chapels.

➢ *Proceed into the cloister [Floor Plan # 10].*

CLOISTER

This late-13th-century cloister is the largest in England. Oddly, it was built for secular clergy, not for monks. Access to the cloister is through the south transept. The traceried windows consist of a large, six-part roundel at the top, supported by a pillar and by two smaller roundels. All the glass is plain. The eastern walkway leads to the chapter house.

➢ *Enter chapter house [Floor Plan #11].*

CHAPTER HOUSE

The chapter house, constructed from 1282–1547, is notable for its octagonal shape, slender central pillar, and decorative medieval frieze. This structure, ac-

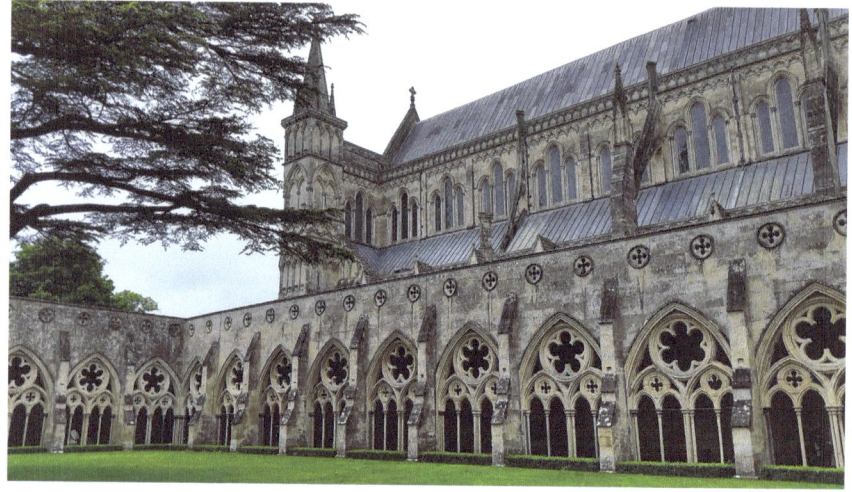

Cloister

cessible from the cloister, was inspired by the one at Westminster Abbey. The central pillar with its eight Purbeck shafts is dramatic as it rises, then divides into 16 branches which support the beautiful vault. Note the large Victorian windows. Below them is a stone arcade, and beneath this a stone bench. There is a raised seat for the bishop and his officials at the east end.

Of special interest is the most elaborate and artistic frieze in the UK, which circles the interior above the arcade and stone bench. It shows scenes and stories from the books of Genesis and Exodus, including Adam and Eve, Noah, the Tower of Babel, and Abraham, Isaac, and Jacob.

Vault and windows

LIBRARY

Situated above the cloister, this 15th-century treasure-trove holds about 5,000 volumes and a valuable collection of manuscripts. Among the most interesting are: a 969 CE version of the Psalter; Geoffrey of Monmouth's Chronicles (12th century); a rare copy of the original Magna Carta (now in the Treasury room). There are also many others of much value and importance.

➤ *Exit via visitor door.*

ANNEX 1 | PRACTICAL INFORMATION FOR VISITORS

Ancient monuments such as Gothic churches are not there just for casual visitors. They are "living and working" spaces for the community and are national treasures. Therefore, community events can be distracting, and scaffolding for renovation or restoration often blocks one's view.

Given the variability of such situations, prospective visitors to a church should check its website in advance. These sites often provide up-to-date information about the opening hours, parking, transportation, the availability of café and lavatory facilities, as well as the music program and other special events.

Visiting Time

Visiting hours and days vary. Regular services and special events—such as school visits and weddings—can affect one's access.

Entrance Fee

These ancient churches are costly to maintain, and unlike France, English churches are largely self-financing. Thus, visitors may expect to pay a modest amount in entry fees and for some tours, for example, guided tower tours. Residents of Britain should check church websites for a way to save on entry fees.

Guided Tours

Mostly volunteers lead the tours and are very good. Most tours are free. Consider taking more than one since each one is different. This provides the opportunity to learn a range of things. Amusingly or frustratingly, sometimes the guides provide contradicting information!

Photography

Policies vary, ranging from not allowing photography at all (Westminster Abbey and Durham) to charging a fee (some enforced, others not), to being totally free. Scaffolding and blocked-off areas are to be expected.

Meals and Snacks

All 13 churches, except King's College Chapel, have cafes, ranging from good to excellent.

Church Shops

All churches have a shop inside. The exception is King's College Chapel whose shop is across the street where visitors buy entrance tickets.

Public Transportation

To visit each church profiled in this book, even those in small towns, public transport, mainly trains, is excellent in terms of ease of use, convenient schedules, and reasonable cost.

ANNEX 2 | GLOSSARY OF TERMS

Church-related Terms

Abbey	A monastery or convent under the spiritual leadership of an abbot or an abbess. A priory differs from an abbey only because the superior bears the title of prior instead of abbot.
Anglican Church	Protestant, consisting of the Church of England and churches which are historically tied to it, including the Episcopal Church in the US.
Basilica	The design of a basilica is Roman in origin, with a nave, apse, and aisles. Now refers to a church given special ceremonial rights by the Pope.
Cathedral	A church holding the bishop's throne, or cathedra; the seat of a bishop.
Church	Any gathering place of Christians for worship.
Church of England	Headed by the Archbishop of Canterbury with the monarch as governor. Formally established as a national church in the 6th century by Augustine of Canterbury. It renounced papal authority when Henry VIII sought to secure an annulment from Catherine of Aragon in the 1530s.
Episcopal Church	The US member church of the Anglican Communion. Established after the American Revolution, when it became separate from the Church of England. The Episcopal Church describes itself as "Protestant, yet Catholic."
Minster	Originally an Anglo-Saxon missionary teaching church, or a church attached to a monastery, but later an honorific title given to certain churches.

Historical Terms

Medieval	A descriptive term for the Middle Ages.
Middle Ages	The period from the fall of Rome (c.500) to c.1350 (or even until 1450/1500 depending on the assumption about beginning of Renaissance). Known also as "The Dark Ages."

Architectural Terms

Ambulatory	The aisle surrounding the choir and high altar, leading to the chapels enclosing the apse.
Apse	Rounded east end.
Arcade	A row of arches supported by piers.
Baldachin	A permanent ornamental canopy above a free-stranding altar or throne.
Barrel vault	Pre-Gothic form of ceiling construction, replaced by Gothic ribbed vaults. A type of vault with a continuous arched surface, resembling the inside of a barrel or tunnel. Also known as a tunnel vault.

Bay	One section of the nave, set off by piers on each side.
Boss	Decorative rounded cap often found at the intersection of ceiling ribs.
Buttress	The most famous type is the flying buttress, but there are many other buttresses which act as structural supports for the walls. The flying buttress is attached to the main vertical buttress, or pier. It "flies" upward to intersect the exterior wall in order to support it.
Capital	Decorative top of a pier or pillar.
Change ringing	The art of playing a set of tuned bells in a controlled manner to produce musical variations.
Chapel	Areas which commemorate a particular saint or for another commemorative purpose. Also referred to as a chantry when it has an altar and was commissioned by a wealthy benefactor.
Chapter house	Room where the priests or monks meet to discuss business.
Chantry	See Chapel
Choir	Area east of the nave with stalls and (usually) an organ. Also spelled quire.
Choir screen	Large screen which divides the east arm of a church from the west, i.e., the nave. Also referred to as the pulpitum or rood screen.
Clerestory	Highest interior elevation.
Cloister	Four covered walkways with a courtyard in the middle that is not covered. The presence of a cloister often indicates that it is (or was once) all or part monastic.
Close	A grassy precinct which often includes other buildings related to the cathedral.
Corbel	Structural piece of stone or wood jutting from a wall to carry a weight. A type of bracket.
Crossing	Where nave, choir, and transept come together.
Crossing tower	Central tower above the crossing.
Crypt	Basement where tombs and relics are often displayed. Also referred to as the Undercroft, when used as a cellar or storage room.
Elevation	Number of interior levels, usually three, including arcade, triforium, and clerestory.
Fan vault	Fan-shaped clusters of tracery-like ribs springing from slender columns or from pendant knobs at the center.
Gable	Triangular area at the top of a portal or façade.
Galilee porch	A chapel or porch at the west front of some churches where penitents waited before admission to the church, and where clergy received women for consultations.

Grisaille window	A window glazed with light-colored or gray glass, rather than bright colors.
Hammer beam	A combination of beams, braces, and rafters that help support a roof's weight. Allowed for higher ceilings while using timber frame construction instead of masonry or stone.
High altar	The holiest part of the church, reserved exclusively for the clergy. The principal altar in a church. The area housing this altar is also referred to as the Presbytery, Chancel, or Sanctuary.
High altar screen	A carved stone or wooden screen, or decoration behind the altar, often including religious screen images, aka a reredos or baldachin.
Lady Chapel	British term for a chapel dedicated to the Virgin Mary.
Lantern	The base of a tower or spire, designed to allow light into the cathedral. A structure with windows above the crossing.
Lancet window	A slender pointed arch shaped like a lance—describes windows or portions of windows.
Lavatorium	The monk's communal washing place in a monastery, typically adjacent to the refectory.
Misericord	Ledge projecting from the underside of a hinged seat in a choir stall. Used by the monks to lean against during the long services, when they were not allowed to sit—aka misereres.
Mullion	Slender shaft or narrow column used to divide a window.
Nave	The long western part of a church with a principal aisle and traditionally with aisles on either side.
Oculus	A round window opening. May have three or four petals in the shape of a trefoil or quatrefoil.
Pier	A support between arcade openings. The massive circular versions are called drum piers. Cruciform (cross-shaped) piers and compound piers are common architectural elements.
Pillar	A non-tapering support, not necessarily cylindrical. May be rectangular, octagonal, or circular, and may have a capital.
Pinnacle	A vertical ornament, pyramidal or conical, crowning a tower or other architectural member. May be capped with a finial.
Pointed arch	One of the three essential elements of Gothic architecture.
Porch	The reception space surrounding a portal. Rarely enclosed in Gothic architecture, except where such a design is used to glorify a transept façade.
Portal	A major entrance, doorway.
Purbeck marble	Marble-like black stone used for the shafts that decorate the stone piers and upper window openings.

Relic	Remains or object associated with a saint.
Ridge rib	A rib which runs down the apex of the vault in a longitudinal direction.
Rose window	Large round window with radial patterns.
Secular clergy	Clergy who were not separated from the world by a written rule or by life in a monastic community; it included the bishops and priests who worked with the laity.
Shaft	Small, often rounded, decoration attached to/clustered around a pier or a window opening. Also used to create a vertical line leading the eye from floor to ceiling.
Spandrel	The space between two arches or between an arch and a rectangular enclosure.
Spire	Tapering structure surmounting a tower. Sometimes the tower itself is designed as a spire. Can be wood, stone, or cast iron.
Stalls	Seating rows on each side of the choir, with benches or seats (misericords) for the clergy.
String course	Decorative horizontal band running around a room.
Tower	A structure, often square, rising above parts of a cathedral, usually over the west front or over the crossing.
Tracery	Stonework with a decorative pattern in windows and wall surfaces.
Transept	The arm that crosses between the nave and choir at a right angle. Each side of the arm may project beyond the cathedral walls, forming the cruciform shape, and terminate in a façade with windows.
Triforium	Middle interior elevation, between the arcade and clerestory.
Tympanum	Triangular area on a façade above a portal. Set between the lintel and the arch above it. Often used for sculpture.
Undercroft	See Crypt
Vault	An arched ceiling. A ribbed vault is comprised of slender diagonal arches or ribs that provide support for the cells of the vault.
Vestry	A room where the clergy and choir dress and the vestments are kept.
Vicar	Priest responsible for the pastoral activity and spiritual care of people in a region.

ANNEX 3 | REFERENCES

Print Sources

Bernard, G.W., *The Dissolution of Monasteries*, History (Journal of the Historical Association), 96 (324): 390-406, Oct 2011

Bygate, J.E. *Bells Cathedrals: The Cathedral Church of Durham*. London: George Bell. 1905

Clifton-Taylor, Alec. *The Cathedrals of England*. London: Thames & Hudson. 1986

Cowan, Painton. *English Stained Glass*. London: Thames & Hudson. 2008

Ditchfield, P.H. *The Cathedrals of Great Britain*. London: J.M. Dent. 1902

Edwards, David L. *The Cathedrals of Britain*. Andover, Hampshire: Pitkin Guides. 1989

Gough, Janet. *Cathedrals of the Church of England*. London: Scala Arts & Heritage Publishers. 2015

Jenkins, Simon. *England's Cathedrals*. London: Little, Brown. 2016

Lehmberg, Stanford E. *The Reformation of Cathedrals*. Princeton, N.J.: Princeton University Press. 1988

Scott, Robert. *The Gothic Enterprise*. Berkeley: U of California Press. 2005.

Sweeting, W.D. *Bells Cathedrals: The Cathedral Church of Ely*. London: George Bell. 1910

_____. *The Cathedral Church of Peterborough*. London: George Bell. 1926

Thurley, Simon. *The Building of England*. London: William Collins. 2013

Plus miscellaneous pamphlets from all churches covered here

Online Sources: Wikipedia and Wikipedia contributors

"Anglo-Saxon architecture," *Wikipedia, The Free Encyclopedia*.
en.wikipedia.org/wiki/Anglo-Saxon architecture (accessed July 2017)

"Anglo-Saxon Settlement of Britain." *Wikipedia, The Free Encyclopedia*.
en.wikipedia.org/wiki/Anglo-Saxon_settlement_of_Britain (accessed July 2017)

"Architecture of the medieval cathedrals of England," *Wikipedia, The Free Encyclopedia*.
en.wikipedia.org/wiki/Architecture_of_the_medieval_cathedrals_of_England (accessed July 2017)

"Canterbury Cathedral," *Wikipedia, The Free Encyclopedia*.
en.wikipedia.org/wiki/Canterbury_Cathedral (accessed July 2017)

"Church and state in medieval Europe," *Wikipedia, The Free Encyclopedia*.
en.wikipedia.org/wiki/Church_and_state_in_medieval_Europe (accessed July 2017)

"Durham Cathedral," *Wikipedia, The Free Encyclopedia*.
en.wikipedia.org/wiki/Durham_Cathedral (accessed July 2017)

"Ely Cathedral," *Wikipedia, The Free Encyclopedia*.
en.wikipedia.org/wiki/Ely_Cathedral (accessed August 2017)

"English Gothic architecture," *Wikipedia, The Free Encyclopedia.*
en.wikipedia.org/wiki/English_Gothic_architecture (accessed August 2017)

"Exeter Cathedral," *Wikipedia, The Free Encyclopedia.*
en.wikipedia.org/wiki/Exeter_Cathedral (accessed August 2017)

"Flying Buttress," *Wikipedia, The Free Encyclopedia.*
en.wikipedia.org/wiki/Flying_buttress (accessed August 2017)

"Gloucester Cathedral," *Wikipedia, The Free Encyclopedia.*
en.wikipedia.org/wiki/Gloucester_Cathedral (accessed September 2017)

"Kings College Chapel, Cambridge," *Wikipedia, The Free Encyclopedia.*
en.wikipedia.org/wiki/King%27s_College_Chapel,_Cambridge (accessed September 2017)

"Lanfranc," *Wikipedia, The Free Encyclopedia.*
en.wikipedia.org/wiki/Lanfranc (accessed September 2017)

"Lincoln Cathedral," *Wikipedia, The Free Encyclopedia.*
en.wikipedia.org/wiki/Lincoln_Cathedral (accessed October 2017)

"Norman architecture," *Wikipedia, The Free Encyclopedia.*
en.wikipedia.org/wiki/Norman_architecture (accessed October 2017)

"Peterborough Cathedral," *Wikipedia, The Free Encyclopedia.*
en.wikipedia.org/wiki/Peterborough_Cathedral (accessed October 2017)

"Religion in Medieval England," *Wikipedia, The Free Encyclopedia.*
en.wikipedia.org/wiki/Religion_in_Medieval_England (accessed October 2017)

"Rib Vault," *Wikipedia, The Free Encyclopedia.*
en.wikipedia.org/wiki/Rib_vault (accessed October 2017)

"Ring of Bells," *Wikipedia, The Free Encyclopedia.*
en.wikipedia.org/wiki/Ring_of_bells (accessed October 2017)

"Salisbury Cathedral," *Wikipedia, The Free Encyclopedia.*
en.wikipedia.org/wiki/Salisbury_Cathedral (accessed November 2017)

"Wells Cathedral," *Wikipedia, The Free Encyclopedia.*
en.wikipedia.org/wiki/Wells_Cathedral (Accessed November 2017)

"Westminster Abbey," *Wikipedia, The Free Encyclopedia.*
en.wikipedia.org/wiki/Westminster_Abbey (accessed December 2017)

"Winchester Cathedral," *Wikipedia, The Free Encyclopedia.*
en.wikipedia.org/wiki/Winchester_Cathedral (accessed December 2017)

"York Cathedral," *Wikipedia, The Free Encyclopedia.*
en.wikipedia.org/wiki/York_Cathedral (Accessed January 2018)

Other Online Sources

Athena Review. "Gothic Architecture." athenapub.com/14gothic-architecture.htm

BBC. "The Cathedrals of Britain." bbc.co.uk/history/british/architecture_cathedral_01.shtml

Cambridge Military History. "The Hedda Stone and Peterborough Abbey."
cambridgemilitaryhistory.com/2014/11/

Cowan, Painton. "The Medieval Stained Glass Photographic Archive." therosewindow.com/

Encyclopedia Brittanica. "Basilica Architecture."
www.britannica.com/technology/basilica-architecture

Hampshire History. "The Shrine of St. Swithun."
www.hampshire-history.com/shrine-of-st-swithun/

Martindale, Andrew, H.R. "Gothic Art and Architecture."
history-world.org/gothic_art_and_architecture.htm

Ross, David, Ed. "English Architecture." Britain Express.
www.britainexpress.com/architecture/index.htm

____. "Exeter Cathedral."Britain Express.
www.britainexpress.com/counties/devon/az/exeter/cathedral.htm

____. "Kings College Chapel Cambridge." Britain Express.
www.britainexpress.com/counties/cambridgeshire/az/cambridge/kings-college-chapel.htm

Sacred Destinations. "Canterbury Cathedral."
www.sacred-destinations.com/england/canterbury-cathedral

____. "Kings College Chapel, Cambridge."
www.sacred-destinations.com/england/cambridge-kings-college-chapel

Image Credits

Page 6 (top first): Ollie Taylor/Dreamstime
Page 19 (top) and all floor plans: ©Nicole Doyle
Page 19 (bottom): ©Richard Moore
Page 29: CL-Medien/Shutterstock.com
Page 33: Luckydoor/Dreamstime
Pages 35, 37, 38, 39, 40: Dean and Chapter of Westminster
Page 42: Claudiodivizia/Dreamstime
Page 48: Constantin Opris/Dreamstime
Page 50 (top): Andrew Howson/Dreamstime
Page 60: Dmitry Naumov/Dreamstime
Page 64 (top): Ron Ellis/Shutterstock.com
Page 67: PlusONE/Shutterstock.com
Page 69: Frank Back/Shutterstock.com
Pages 74, 76: ©Barbara Beach
Page 78: Ron Ellis/Shutterstock.com
Page 82: Phillip Bird/Dreamstime
Page 85 (top right): Leifr/Dreamstime
Page 88: Graham Taylor/Dreamstime

Page 89 (top): Angelina Dimitrova/Shutterstock.com
Page 108 (top): Adrian Carley/Dreamstime
Page 112: Tonybrindley/Dreamstime
Page 116: Ionut David/Dreamstime
Page 121 (top): Alexey Lebedev/Dreamstime
Page 123 (left): Fernando Carniel Machado/Dreamstime
Page 124: Emily Marie Wilson/Shutterstock.com
Page 128: Stocksre/Shutterstock.com
Page 129: Sue Martin/Dreamstime
Pages 133, 135, 136, 138: Peter Lowis
Page 147 (top): Jacek Ojnarowski/Shutterstock.com
Page 149 (top): Andrew Emptage/Dreamstime
Page 150: A G Baxter/Shutterstock.com
Page 172: ©Richard Moore
Page 176: Graham Taylor/Dreamstime

The photos not listed above, including the cover, are by ©Sawon Hong.

ACKNOWLEDGMENTS

It affords a particular pleasure for us to acknowledge and thank the many friends who helped make this book possible. We received valuable comments and suggestions on the earlier draft from Barbara and Lee R. Beach, Charlotte Cromer, Mary Doyle, David Feigin, Jerry Huguet, Eva Jespersen, Timothy Johnson, and Ja-Kyung Yoo. We are especially grateful to Asta Kenney, Diana King, Gretta Powers, and Elizabeth Simon for their thorough review of the manuscript and for factual and editorial insights which greatly improved the manuscript. We also wish to offer our special thanks to Nicole Doyle for her expert graphics, and to Peter Lowis, Chapter Photographer of Durham Cathedral, for his generous contribution of the fine photos of this cathedral. Not least, the book has benefited a great deal from the design work of Sheila Johnston Sherer.

ABOUT THE AUTHORS

Richard Moore

Retired after over forty years in international development work. He received a PhD in international management from Cornell University, and has an MFA in writing. His essays have appeared in many literary magazines, including *Fine Arts Connoisseur*. He taught a course on French Gothic Cathedrals at the Encore Learning program in Virginia, and has lectured on these architectural monuments in the Washington, DC area.

Sawon Hong

Retired from UNICEF, she has PhD in Sociology from the University of Hawaii. She has also published the book, *A Nomadic Life,* based upon her first-hand experiences working and living overseas.

The authors also published *Guidebook: Selected French Gothic Cathedrals and Churches* (AuthorHouse) in 2016.

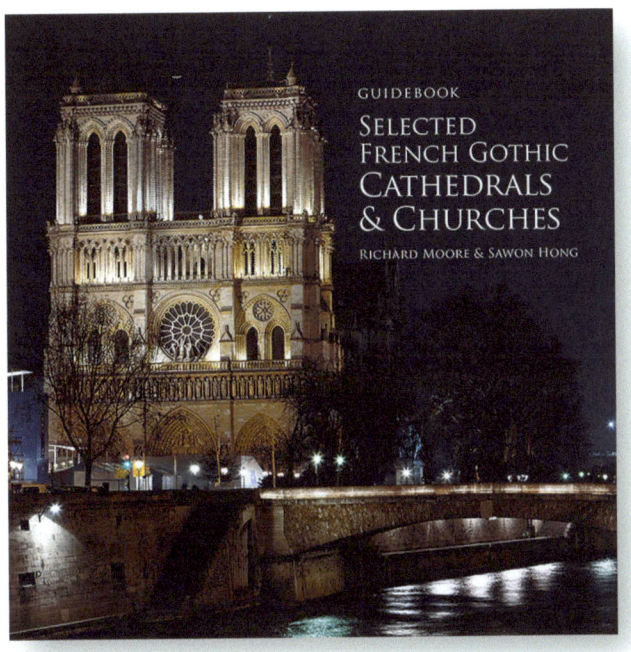

BY THE SAME AUTHORS

Guidebook
Selected French Gothic Cathedrals & Churches

2016 | AuthorHouse

www.ingramcontent.com/pod-product-compliance
Lightning Source LLC
Chambersburg PA
CBHW041351290426
44108CB00001B/11